Jezebels Whoredoms, Perversions and Witchcrafts

"Ancient darkness corrupting the 21st century church"

Apostle Robert Summers

Jezebels Whoredoms, Perversions and Witchcrafts

**Published by
Summers Ministries
Columbus, Ohio**

Jezebels Whoredoms, Perversions and Witchcrafts

Copyright 2016 by Apostle Robert Summers
All rights reserved

No part of this book may be reproduced, stored in a retrieval system, or transcribed in any for or by any means, electronic or mechanical, including photocopying and recording, without prior written permission of Apostle Robert Summers, Sr. or Summers Ministries.

Unless otherwise indicated, all scriptures used are from the King James Version Bible

Cover Design by: CI-Media

Printed in USA

Dedication

This book is dedicated to my son John Summers who has a heart of gold and refuses to operate under the status quo in life. John, you are a true pioneer and an extraordinary person. I love and appreciate you.

Acknowledgements

I would like to express my appreciation to the following people who made this project possible.

First, to my wife Dixie, who always supports and encourages me to keep doing what God told me to do. Bae, I love you more than life itself. You are such a blessing and I could not be who I am without you.

To my children Kimberly, Kenya (Bryan), Kenneth, Rob (Emelie), John, David and Mikey who patiently shared me with others. You have given up countless hours of "Dad time." Thank you for your love and support during rough times.

To Apostle John Eckhardt and Prophetess Wanda Eckhardt for being great spiritual parents. Your support, encouragement, impartation and love are extremely valuable. Thank you for recognizing God's call and purpose in my live.

Finally, to my spiritual sons and daughters, friends, and family members who support Summers Ministries and the vision God has given me – thank you.

Table of Contents

Introduction

Section One ….……….. Jezebel's Whoredoms

Section Two …………… Jezebel's Perversions

Section Three …..…….... Jezebel's Witchcrafts

Introduction

It is without question, that the Jezebel spirit is the most notoriously sinister spirit that operates in the church and world today. This ancient spirit has been at the helm of orchestrating the demise of nations, races, churches ministries and families for ages. It is sly, cunning and is capable of deceiving mass people groups. It is a spirit that understands how to effectively maneuver within systems to gain power within. This includes the secular world, the religious church, and what is commonly known as the apostolic-prophetic church. There is no place that Jezebel will not attempt to spin her web of destruction in. The only exception to this statement is the Kingdom of God. The Kingdom is unshakeable and rules over all.

Jezebel perpetrates systems through releasing her witchcraft, whoredoms and perversions. Unfortunately today many do not comprehend Jezebel's mission, strategies and operation. This plays nicely into Jezebels carnage of those ignorant of her cunning devises.

My wife and I have battled and contended with the spirit of Jezebel in ministry, family and business for over several decades. There have been times where we were blind-sided by this insidious spirit. In other times, we fell victim to her deception and became weary and worn out. We have experienced extensive collateral damage and frustration; however we have always come out of these battles stronger and more educated relative to how to contend with Jezebel's evil plots. Perhaps one of the reasons why many consider us as experts in the arena of battling Jezebel is because we have been tempered through enduring the tribulations of Jezebel. The key to winning these battles has always been to not tolerate or sympathize with the host that harbors this spirit.

But I have this against you: that you tolerate the woman Jezebel, who calls herself a prophetess [claiming to be inspired], and who is teaching and leading astray my servants and beguiling them into practicing sexual vice and eating food sacrificed to idols – Revelation 2:20 (Amplified Version)

The 21st century church is just like the church in Thyatira. It has a lot going on. Impressive crowds, numerous activities, around the clock prayer, strong benevolent programs and new converts are constantly coming into the Kingdom. Yet, similar to its 1st century counterpart, it tolerates and gives room for Jezebel to operate. Either in their presence or in leadership themselves, the church at large has tolerated the Jezebel spirit.

To tolerate something is to: "allow the existence, occurrence, or practice of something that one does not necessarily like or agree with. It is to permit something without interference or to accept or endure (someone or something unpleasant or disliked) with forbearance."

Today, society has become extremely tolerant. It is so tolerant that a good portion of people is afraid to voice their true opinions and convictions for the fear of offending or upsetting someone. They're afraid of being rejected for sharing their views or worse yet, of being labeled as someone that does not love others. Tolerance of wickedness will always result in societal decay.

Wickedness can be defined as a "departure from the rules of the divine law; evil disposition or practices; immorality; crime; sin; sinfulness; and corrupt manners.

Wickedness generally signifies evil practices. The spirit of Jezebel is a wicked spirit that stirs up a complacent, slothful and tolerant spirit in those she seduces.

But there was none like unto Ahab, which did sell himself to work wickedness in the sight of the Lord, whom Jezebel his wife stirred up – I Kings 21:25

King Ahab was tolerant of his wife's Jezebel's whoredoms and witchcrafts. When Jezebel came to Israel, she brought with her the pagan god Baal. While King Ahab undoubtedly knew this was a direct violation of the commandment of Jehovah, he quickly begins erecting sanctuaries for Baal.

And it came to pass, as if it had been a light thing for him to walk in the sins of Jeroboam the son of Nebat, that he took to wife Jezebel the daughter of Ethbaal king of the Zidonians, and went and served Baal, and worshipped him. And he reared up an altar for Baal in the house of Baal, which he had built in Samaria. And Ahab made a grove; and Ahab did more to provoke the Lord God of Israel to anger than all the kings of Israel that were before him - 1 Kings 16:31-33

Jezebel did not accept Ahab's God - Jehovah, but rather she seduces Ahab to tolerate Baal-worship. Jezebel's seduction will always lead to a place of tolerance. Once you tolerate Jezebel you will be affected by her whoredoms, witchcrafts and perversions - without exception.

When government and/or it's people become tolerant of the perverse ideologies or actions that oppose the law and rule of the kingdom of God, or go against the moral fabric of biblical truth's – Jezebel will be found sitting on the seat of authority over that nation. However, it does not stop there. This tolerance cascades its way into families, marriages, churches, business and ultimately every sector of society.

One of the greatest problems that exist in the church today is the attempt to normalize dysfunction. When dysfunction becomes acceptable, Jezebel has full range of motion to establish her network – undaunted.

Families and churches are filled with Jezebels perversion and whoredoms. Her witchcrafts are out of control and consistently progress to new levels, while the average Christian simply meanders along playing the religious game it's become accustomed to – attend church on Sunday, and feed the flesh the rest of the week.

The Church, specifically in the United States, expends an enormous amount of time, energy and money engaging in activities that yield limited to no measurable results. Of course every church, ministry, network and denomination boasts of its cutting edge training in areas ranging from the Apostolic to the Prophetic. Unquestionably, we are very good at applauding our own actions. Our gatherings and meetings are always '"powerful." The anointing is so thick you can almost cut it with a knife, and the glory – well, it's so heavy that we can barely stand. Enthusiastically, we claim to have "watchers" over cities and intercessors that fight off demonic spirits from having their way, while others sleep peacefully. We have Prophets that engage in atmospheric warfare, apostolic generals that direct the flow of spiritual traffic in (what's termed as) "their territories," and deliverance ministers that can identify a demons name and ranking.

Yet one look at society at-large and we clearly see these subjective measurements as non-existent. Visit the home of some "believers" or get to know them outside a church environment and you'll see a family, marriage and individual that although attempts desperately to cover up their dysfunction with religious clutter, is living in a world of confusion, chaos and misery. Assess the character of many religious leaders rather than idolizing them and you'll discover just how deep the rabbit hole of Jezebel's wicked network goes. Sadly at the core of many Christian families and churches today is *"Jezebel's Whoredoms, Perversions and Witchcrafts."*

Jezebel's **whoredom** refers to betrayal, unfaithfulness and breaking of covenant. Additionally, false covenants in the form of alliances and confederacies to religious systems are whoredoms.

The entire book of Hosea is about Israel's worship of idols, which to God was an act of adultery against Him because; He was in covenant relationship with them. God was married to Israel.

*They will not frame their doings to turn unto their God: for the spirit of **whoredoms** is in the midst of them, and they have not known the Lord. Hosea 5:4*

*They do not direct their deeds toward turning to God, for the spirit of **harlotry** is in their midst Hosea 5:4 (NKJV)*

The two terms used here are "Whoredoms" *(KJV)* and "Harlotry." *(NKJV)*

The word harlotry essentially means "adultery, fornication and prostitution." But the word harlotry takes on a greater meaning spiritually. It means idolatry, spiritual adultery, or unfaithfulness.

Perversions are embedded in Jezebel's nature. However, when talking about her perversions, one typically thinks in terms of perverse sexuality. While this is true in part, it only provides a shadow of understanding to how her evil network has invaded our churches and families. The perversions of Jezebel have more to do with her corruptions and false identities that she establishes within the minds of her prey. A Jezebelic mindset is perverted thinking that plays out in churches according to her agenda.

They can't think straight anymore. Feeling no pain, they let themselves go in sexual obsession, addicted to every sort of **perversion** *– Ephesians 4:19 (Message Bible)*

Finally, Jezebels **witchcrafts** are many. The mighty warrior Jehu mentions both the whoredom and witchcraft of Jezebel.

"And it came to pass when Joram saw Jehu that he said, 'Is it peace, Jehu?' And he answered, 'What peace so

*long as the whoredom of thy mother **Jezebel** and her **witchcraft** are so many?'"* - *2 Kings 9:22*

Witchcraft is in the church. The problem is most church leaders and certainly most Believers don't understand what witchcraft is. They're comprehension of spiritual warfare and deliverance ministry is either shallow or erroneous. Witchcraft is an ancient spirit that has penetrated the *ecclesia* through the lust of the flesh. It disguises itself, and operates in stealth like manner typically as an ultra-spiritualist.

Jezebels network is vast and is more pronounced than you may think. Jezebels Empire is highly organized, well funded, and grossly intelligent and has recruiting tools that lures many into its program. I've have found that this spirit has much invested in churches, leaders, believers and families everywhere. Jezebel's network is a network of perverse thoughts that introduce whoredoms and partner with the flesh. The flesh is witchcraft and today we find many believers are fulfilling the lust of their flesh rather than walking in the spirit. Her ability to deceive believers into thinking they're walking (living) in the spirit is defined by one of her greatest accomplishment ever – the Religious Institution.

Jesus did not come to establish or bring a religion. He came to bring that which man lost – The Kingdom of Heaven. Jesus greatest opposition came from the religious leaders of

His day. The religious spirit is a murdering spirit that killed the Prophets of God and the Lord Jesus.

One of the greatest tools of Jezebel is religion. Jezebel was (and that spirit is) religious. Religion is man's attempt to find God. It unilaterally results in idolatry. It is the nucleus of racism and its strength is found in the traditions of men. It replaces liberty with legalism and the power of God with sensationalism. Jezebel has built many religious temples and positioned her priests to oversee its idolatrous worship. This religious spirit has bewitched many believers and has them entangled in Jezebels vicious web of destruction. Rather than getting equipped in the things of the Kingdom, they have been entertained in circus like environments that pamper to the flesh. Many religious churches are nothing more than adult day-care centers that sedate followers through a one man only - hour of power service.

Jezebels religious network of whoredom, perversion and witchcraft has systematically released her false doctrine of demons. Today, many believers read the scriptures through a religious lens that has them blind to the truth. A deceived believer is an unstable believer that will never excel in life. The hallmark of the religious spirit is creating schizophrenic followers. As it was in the 1st century when one minute the people cried, *"Hosanna to the highest!"* yet in another breath they yelled, *"Crucify Him,"* So it is today with many that have taken offense, embraced rejection and operate in rebellion (witchcraft.) They call Jesus Lord yet they will not do what the He says. Rather, they do what their religious ideology, denomination or Bishop says. They sing of His love, yet will stab you in the back when you expose their perversion. One minute they're with you, and the next they want to kill you. This is the nature of the Spirit of Jezebel. She's a ruthless murdering spirit that will not be satisfied until she has destroyed families, marriages, ministries, lives and generations.

Why I wrote this book

This book is the sequel to *"Harboring the Spirit of Jezebel – Caught in the web of Destruction."* In that book I explained the principal targets, suspects and retaliatory responses of Jezebel when she is exposed. In this book, my purpose is to expose some of Jezebels strategies, methods and operations specifically within the church. Together, we will explore Jezebels counterfeiting methods, her theatrical performances, perverse characteristics and unique tactics she implements in establishing a stronghold.

Most people in the Church can identify some of Jezebels characteristics. Two of the most common are Control and Manipulation. But this spirit is much more complex than these two identifiers. Admittedly, many people have abused and overly utilized the term Jezebel or Jezebel spirit. Excessive and indiscriminate use of the term can detract from properly discerning and analyzing the characteristics and modus operandi of this wicked spirit. It can also discredit genuine deliverance ministry. Therefore we must remain true to scripture pertaining to our knowledge of this spirit. Further, within the deliverance ministry ranks, we must operate professionally and with standards that ensure we do not diagnose every issue as being Jezebel. We must move away from the religious labels of old which have nothing to do with this spirit and progress towards the potential association it has with the various clinical diagnoses found within the mental health arena, specifically, Narcissistic Personality Disorder, Paranoid Personality Disorder, Anxiety Disorders, Split Identity Disorder and Dissociative Identity Disorder.

Nevertheless, the fact remains that the Spirit of Jezebel can be seen in the majority of local churches, and the average leader is either ill equipped or simply refuses to address it. Sadly, many are afraid to address it or they resort to non-confrontational methods that undoubtedly play nicely into Jezebels campaign to secure a stronghold. This is where this book will add the greatest value - Understanding how to identify Jezebels embedded activities in the church; it's leaders and participants.

This book is one book in a series of writings on the topic of Jezebel. Undoubtedly, we're unable to cover every feature, attribute, and characteristic of the Jezebel spirit. Nor are we capable of addressing every question you may have. Therefore, we will purposefully and intentionally release quality resources in a timely manner.

It is my prayer that this book will further equip you to gain freedom from the many years of pain, frustration and harm that you experienced at the hand of Jezebel. I believe your eyes will be opened as we reveal just how cunning and crafty this spirit is within the local church. You will be challenged to change your mindset on things; specifically those things we think are right but are really a part of Jezebels network. Those currently caught in Jezebel's religious web will feel the pressure as religious strongholds, ideologies, and disorder all get shook up.

For those that are capable of loosing the cords of Jezzy's tangled web, be encouraged. As you receive your emancipation from Jezebels web of destruction, you will be strengthened to rise up and with boldness declare that Jezebels – *Whoredoms, Perversions and Witchcraft* will be tolerated in your life………………………..No more!

Section One
Jezebels Whoredoms

When people hear the term *"whoredom"* they typically think of prostitution. The King James Version of the bible uses the word "whoredom" whereas the New King James Version utilizes the word *"harlotry."*

Harlotry speaks of idolatry, adultery and unfaithfulness. In the 21st century, many believers, churches, ministries and leaders ignorantly engage in "spiritual harlotry.

And it came to pass when Joram saw Jehu that he said, 'Is it peace, Jehu?' And he answered, 'What peace so long as the <u>whoredom</u> of thy mother Jezebel and her witchcraft are so many?' -2 Kings 9:22

Whoredom can be easily defined as idolatry. Other words associated with whoredom are; adultery, fornication and prostitution. Jezebel is the Queen of all whoredom. This spirit is one that seeks to worship everything and anything except the only true God.

Harlotry was a prime characteristic of Jezebel who lived in the 9th century BC. Jezebel was a priestess under the tutelage of her father, Ethbaal. Ethbaal was king of the Phoenicians, a group whose ancestors were the Canaanites. The Phoenicians worshipped many gods and goddesses, chiefly among them Baal.

In the Bible we see Jezebel wedding herself to the wicked leader of Israel – Ahab. She quickly moved to introduce idolatry into his life as an evil religious practice. This union, between Ahab and Jezebel was not a marriage of love. Rather, it was a religious and political affiliation designed to eradicate true worship from Israel. Not only was Jezebel determined to eliminate all worship of the only true God, she hastily moved to kill most of God's genuine prophets and then, ordained her false prophets of Baal and Asherah.

Jezebel successfully controlled Ahab and implemented idol worship. She also had Ahab build her a temple for idol worship.

And it came to pass, as if it had been a light thing for him to walk in the sins of Jeroboam the son of Nebat, that he took to wife Jezebel the daughter of Ethbaal king of the Zidonians, and went and served Baal, and worshipped him. And he reared up an altar for Baal in the house of Baal, which he had built in Samaria. And Ahab made a grove; and Ahab did more to provoke the Lord God of Israel to anger than all the kings of Israel that were before him – I Kings 16:31-33

Jezebel should have accepted Ahab's (Israel's) God but she did not. Rather, through her harlotry she leads King Ahab to a place of tolerance. Clearly one of the greatest challenges we face today in the 21st century church is being tolerant of that which takes our minds off the things of the Kingdom and places them on the things of the flesh.

In many ways the church, like Israel has played the harlot.

……… they shall play the harlot and beget no increase, because they have forsaken the Lord for harlotry; Harlotry and wine and new wine take away the heart and the mind and the spiritual understanding – Hosea 4:10(b)

The apostasy of Israel prepared the way for her whoredoms. Today it is the carnival like performance of preachers, ministries and churches that is enablers to Jezebels toxic tricks and keeps the minds of believers void of understanding.

Jezebel desires to have believers within the Church worship her gods. She is strategic and cunning in her methods of getting the saints to engage in idolatrous activities. One of those activities is – **worship**. Unfortunately in the church today many are worshipping out of the flesh rather than in the Spirit. In the book of John, Jesus said ….

"But the hour is coming, and is now here, when the true worshipers will worship the Father in spirit and truth, for the Father is seeking such people to worship him. God is spirit, and those who worship him must worship in spirit and truth." - John 4:23-24 (ESV)

I'm certain you would agree that many of our gatherings and church meetings have evolved into nothing short of circus-type entertainment assemblies. Our churches are becoming spiritual health clubs, outlets for exercising emotions, feelings and euphoria. There's very little, if any Doctrine of Christ and His Kingdom. There's no stand taken against perversion, witchcraft or idolatry. Much of it is vain *(empty)* worship.

This people draweth nigh unto me with their mouth, and honoureth me with their lips; but their heart is far from me. But in vain they do worship me – Matthew 15:8

The Jezebel spirit will look to entertain you rather than enable you to worship in **SPIRIT** and in **TRUTH**. This is true regardless of what associative banner one sails under. Whether Charismatic, Pentecostal, Apostolic and Prophetic, or some other denomination or network, much of the worship today is motivated by the flesh and orchestrated by Jezebel. Clearly this doesn't hold true for all churches. Many churches are highly autonomous and are not "boxed in" to a particular way to worship, so I want to be careful not to paint them all with the same broad brush. However, the fact is that many church services and gatherings have subscribed to a religious order and model that has galvanized their followers into thinking that - what they do is how it should be done everywhere.

Think for a moment how the typical assembly or gathering operates today, specifically, in the western world. Although some don't want to admit it, generally there is what's called an "order of service." The typical order goes something like this: praise and worship, announcements, offering, sermon, prayer and closing of service or benediction. Certainly there are variations, but this is usually what takes place.

Now let's take for example what commonly occurs in Apostolic – Prophetic churches. The general layout is basically the same. The only exception is that the service may open up with declarations and decrees and end with prayer and ministry to the corporate body. While this is certainly a refreshing improvement from some of the more "stale" services that exist, could it be that this "model" keeps the collective body boxed in also? Could it be that Jezebel has embedded herself in what many call the heavenly model or sound of heaven? And could it be that a model has been created that mesmerizes the people to watch a show and idolize the showmen? Could it be that we're idolizing our own subscriptions and in effect, worshiping outwardly but hearts are far from Him?

Personally I embrace the apostolic and prophetic dimension of the church. However I understand that the spirit of Jezebel devotes itself to hanging out in these type ministries and corporate gatherings. Let us not forget that Jezebel hates proper structure. The apostolic dimension of the church is foundational or structural. The apostolic is the dimension we see believers in the 1st century operating in. The Church is built (established) upon the foundation of the apostles & prophets.

> *And are built upon the foundation of the apostles and prophets, Jesus Christ himself being the chief corner stone*
> *- Ephesians 2:20*

So, it's no wonder why Jezebel invades apostolic ministry. But how does she secure such a vast stronghold in churches, ministries and the lives of believers? Clearly she doesn't come overtly. Rather she navigates her treacheries of whoredom in a covert manner. Two of her primary ways is through *entertainment* and *leadership*. Let's glance at these two areas in more detail.

Entertainment

Let's will look at the entertainment component first. The word entertain can be defined as follows:

- To hold the attention of (someone) with something amusing or diverting - to amuse.
- To extend hospitality toward: *entertain friends at dinner.*
- To consider; contemplate: *entertain an idea.*
- To hold in mind; harbor.

There is a growing trend toward entertainment to fill seats and grow churches and it seems to have nothing to do with Jesus' mission for the church. Today, religious culture, specifically in the United States, has an enormous appetite to be entertained. Some churches, ministries and movements are now catering to the public's desire for 'around the clock' entertainment. A large number of churches are now consumed by a need to fulfill this desire. Many church services and gatherings have such a focus on the praise and worship portion of the event that by the time the Word of God comes forth, people begin to leave or are exhausted. Clearly a spirit that brings people into an emotional frenzy and idolatrous behavior has hijacked the praise and worship segment of these services.

Now before we move forward, please understand that I'm not criticizing the entertainment industry or the time of worship that exists in a local church or gathering. Worship is the lifeblood of the believer and God seeks for the true worshipper. However, God isn't looking for performances but for true worship.

Regarding the arts and entertainment sector, this is a sector that believers should engage and ultimately influence with the Kingdom of Heaven. Unfortunately, religious personnel has historically been fearful of supporting individuals that demonstrate the God given talent to reveal what un-perverted entertainment actually looks like. Hence, rather than equipping the saints with the word of God and releasing them into the world to influence it through serving their gift in it, they demonize the entire sector and become enablers to Jezebel's perversion through avoidance. Not only does this tactic backfire, but also plays nicely into Jezebel trickery. Let me explain.

Whatever is in a person's heart and mind is what they will gravitate to, and ultimately attract. Let's take an example of an individual that has "entertainment" in their heart or mind. They're somewhat gifted in that area and desires to provide "entertainment" to the world at-large. Historically the religious culture would suggest that they could not serve that gift to the world (although God would be glorified through it) because the world is evil and perverted. This is where Jezebel gets in and capitalizes on a religious ideology and culture.

As time progresses, the local church or ministry will eventually use the gift, perhaps making the person part of the praise team or worship leader. Because every gift needs to be released by the vessel that has the gift, they begin to "entertain" the people. Remember people will naturally seek after and attract what they desire. Giving someone a position or title of worship leader or psalmist does not change the heart or mind.

Many praise and worship leaders or team members are actually "entertainers." And it's not the individual entertaining that's doing anything wrong. Remember, they're simply releasing the gift of entertainment that's in them. It's the effect that it has on the people being entertained.

To entertain means to hold one's mind or to harbor. A harbor is a place of anchoring or place of refuge. Spiritually, God never intended entertainment to be a place of refuge. Our refuge is to be in God Himself.

God is our refuge and strength, a very present help in trouble – Psalms 46:1

In God is my salvation and my glory: the rock of my strength, and my refuge, is in God – Psalms 62:7

I will say of the Lord, He is my refuge and my fortress. – Psalms 91:2

Our church services and gatherings are not to be a time where we amuse people or captivate their minds. But that's precisely what entertainment does. Again, there is nothing wrong with entertainment; it's just out of place. Consider for example that there is nowhere in the New Testament church where you see entertainment or concert style gatherings like we have today. As a matter of fact, Paul tells the Corinthian church what to do when they gather together for worship:

*So here's what I want you to do. When you gather for worship, each one of you be prepared with something that will be useful for all: Sing a hymn, teach a lesson, tell a story, lead a prayer, provide an insight. If prayers are offered in tongues, two or three's the limit, and then only if someone is present who can interpret what you're saying. Otherwise, keep it between God and yourself. And no more than two or three speakers at a meeting, with the rest of you listening and taking it to heart. Take your turn, **no one person taking over.** Then each speaker gets a chance to say something special from God, and you all learn from each other. If you choose to speak, you're also responsible for how and when you speak. When we worship the right way, God doesn't stir us up into confusion; he brings us into harmony. This goes for all the churches—**no exceptions** – I Corinthians 14: 26-33 (The Message Bible) (emphasis the author)*

What a powerful passage of scripture. Notice the paradigm is not a worship service that has a select few engaging while others sit back and watch in amazement. No! Rather we see a diverse set of activities being release by everyone. Paul states that everyone should come into the gathering with something they have in them that is useful for all. This is a far cry from our gatherings and worship services we have today.

Worship should never be based on a formula or model. This can move us to idolize our songs and to focus too much on what we're singing and how things sound, all without a real spiritual connection with God. Don't get me wrong, I love worship songs and I certainly have my favorites, but I want to make certain I sincerely mean the things I sing, and that my worship is just not a formulaic effort to win His love, gain position or soothe the flesh.

So what's the problem?

Jezebel's whoredoms and idolatries have navigated their way into the church through entertainment. Today, praise and worship leaders, singers, praise bands and teams are viewed as "highly anointed worshippers" that are vital to the success of any church or event. What better way to pack a local church or enormous auditoriums than to offer a 60 minute praise show performed by an 'entertainer' and enhance it with state-of-the-art sound, lighting, fog machine and video systems.

Now, remember I said earlier: "people will continue to seek after and attract what they desire." Well, could it be that this is exactly what is in the heart of some believers? Could it be that they have opened the doorway for Jezebel to release her idolatry upon the church? Unequivocally yes!

Many people in the church today, while spiritually regenerated, still have their minds in an un-renewed condition. As such, their incredible appetite for entertainment, specifically towards things that are either worldly or culturally relevant to the religious vein they're accustomed to, remains unfulfilled. The bottom line is <u>they are attracted</u> to "entertainment" and have become caught up in a culture that idolizes both the art and the artist.

Let's face it; believers are moviegoers, TV-viewers, music lovers, concert-attendees, sports fans, game enthusiasts, Internet junkies and users of all sorts of other high tech gadgets. And while this is not bad in and of itself, Jezebel will certainly use the lust for entertainment to infiltrate the church with her whoredoms. Increasingly I've found that those who profess Christ and hold to the authority of the scriptures are among those most addicted to this kind of entertainment. To feed their addiction, many simply come to church to attend *"the performance"* principally for the entertainment value.

When it comes to entertainment, church leaders and professing believers need only ask: would Jesus be pleased? Sure, some may say, *"it's all about Him."* Oh really? Seriously, are we going to try to convince ourselves that Sunday morning worship or the 60 minutes of praise was about Him? Have you ever notice that during the praise and worship portion of services that the majority of people stand (or sit) by idly watching as a few others obey the commands of the 'leaders' to clap, raise hands, shout and dance. And what about the dancers? While they say 'their worshipping,' is seems most of the attention is on them and their paraphernalia. I've heard many say that these times are "so glorious' yet if you remove all of the peripherals, let's see just how glorious it truly is. The glory of God is not about outward demonstrations and man-made entertainment, but it's by the Spirit and the Fathers' magnificent power.

Do we need praise and worship? Absolutely. But what we need is genuine praise and worship not theatrical performances in entertainment centers where Jezebel sits on the seat of authority. Worship is about Him, not us. It must be directed at the King of Glory and not our idols that we've raised up. Whether a style, an artist, a song, an atmosphere, and a sound – it's not about any of that. It's about Him!!!!!

Leaders & Polished Showmen

The other element that Jezebel is able to release her whoredoms through is – Leadership. Apostles, Prophets, Evangelists, Pastors, Teachers and leaders are fundamental for the equipping of the saints. Leadership is influence, nothing more, nothing less. Without sound leadership the church will never be influential in society.

John Maxwell states, *"Everything rises and falls on leadership."* Dr. Myles Munroe wrote, *"Nothing happens without leadership."* Clearly, leadership is vitally important to the success of the mission, movement and momentum of the church. Of course, anything that is that important will become a target for Jezebel to destroy.

All leadership must be credible. Without credibility the leaders words have no value. Much goes into the equation of being a credible leader. Clearly, the character of the leader is paramount in determining the ultimate success of that leader. Unfortunately today, many followers focus on the leaders ability or gift. They are followed, not for the content of their character, but rather for their charismatic personality and ability to move people emotionally. Jezebel exploits this as she gets the leader to become filled with pride. They become like King Herod, high-minded, pompous and arrogant.

And upon a set day Herod, arrayed in royal apparel, sat upon his throne, and made an oration unto them. And the people gave a shout, saying, It is the voice of a god, and not of a man. And immediately the angel of the Lord smote him, because he gave not God the glory: and he was eaten of worms, and gave up the ghost – Acts 12:21-23

Today we find many leaders positioning themselves as '*golden calves,*' looking to be idolized and served. This is a classic Jezebel characteristic and trait. The name Jezebel means 'without co-habitation.' It is a spirit that shares worship with no one. Jezebel serves no one but rather expects others to serve her. As such, leaders that are bound by a Jezebel spirit will attract servants rather than disciples.

Many believers have become spiritual groupies following their favorite preacher simply due to his or her ability to captivate an audience. Essentially they have become *"eunuchs"* serving in Jezebels bedchamber.

Jesus said that if one desires to be great in the Kingdom, they must serve.

But Jesus called them to him and said; "You know that the rulers of the Gentiles lord it over them, and their great ones exercise authority over them. It shall not be so among you. But whoever would be great among you must be your servant, and whoever would be first among you must be your slave, even as the Son of Man came not to be served but to serve – Matthew 20:25-28

How many church leaders do you know that serve those they're connected to? That said, how many church leaders actually "connect" with the saints to which they're to serve?

Great leaders are those that SERVE others and foster RELATIONSHIPS with their disciples. Today we see a different picture in the church. We see leaders that are untouchable, isolated and protected. We see leaders that look to be served by their followers rather than serve. We see leaders that seek numbers but do not develop relationships with their followers. We see leaders that take pictures with people; even calling them "sons" or "daughters" yet spend no measurable time with them.

We need leaders that have values, morals, ethics and principles that align with the Kingdom of God and His Word. What we don't need is polished showmen. A **polished showman** typically:

- Displays the religious look and sound
- Is a deceitful stage actor
- Stays up-to-date of the current religious fashion, dress, protocols, buzzwords, terminology and technology.
- Inflates their image and public personality
- Relishes their own press
- Rides on the backs of other leaders, using their name, status, notoriety and success to elevate their personal ministry.
- Navigates every angle to gain access to a stage and platform
- Entertains and mesmerizes their followers through theatrical performances

Many of these polished showmen have become idols in and of themselves. They have become like Ahab and bought into Jezebel's entertainment idols. I've seen certain preachers invited to be the keynote speaker at conferences prancing around as a celebrity pop artist at a concert. I've witnessed preachers perform at epic levels whereby the audience jumps, shouts, high-fives their neighbor, slaps them upside the head and in a frenzy runs down to the stage and slams hundreds of dollars at their feet – yet they have no substance or doctrinal accuracy to their preaching. And then when they're finished holding the people captive for hours, they are ushered off the stage and exit the room like a boxer with their entourage of armor bearers. The saddest part of this is that the majority of the people simply adore it, and keeps coming back for more.

They love the entertainment and excitement. They have gravitated to the celebrity status of their favorite preacher, church or network. They have turned from worshiping the creator to idolizing the creativity of the created.

Today there is an excited interest in peripheral subjects and objects that are not central to the gospel of the Kingdom. Esoteric teachings, writings and prophetic messages that show a greater interest in peripheral topics should be avoided. However, people continue to flock to leaders and ministries that place a focus on these things.

Consider for example flag waving, liturgical dancers, or performances by choirs. Again, and allow me to be crystal clear here, no one is saying these things are bad. Personally, I enjoy the entertainment quality and artistic value they offer. But truthfully, does flag waving, singing or dances choreographed by trained personnel bring one into the presence of God? From a New Testament and Kingdom-minded perspective it doesn't. God's word says if you're a son of God you're perpetually in God's glory and His glory is in you. There's nothing you need to do. It is a spiritual reality. (*2 Cor 3:18, Rom 8:17, I Peter 5:10, I Thess 2:12, John 17:22*).

So why do so many place such a huge emphasis on these things? Yet place very little emphasis on education, specifically equipping the saints, the Charismata, healings, deliverance and the Kingdom?

I cannot stress enough that I'm not against these things. They have their place. We do them in my church. But we must cease from elevating them whereby they de-emphasize the central themes of the gospel.

Many leaders and those that follow their esoteric teachings or razzle-dazzle performances may claim they agree with the gospel, but the bulk of their teachings, writings and prophetic artistry show a greater interest in peripheral topics, novelties and new revelation rather than the foundational truths of the <u>WORD OF GOD</u>, specifically the New Covenant. Anytime we place so much focus on the vessel engaged in these activities, rather than the one who gives the gift, we make it idolatry.

Frankly, leaders and followers alike have embraced Jezebel's sorceries. They have eaten at her table and partaken of the bread of idolatry. Worse yet, many are actually sharing this idolatry with the rest of the body.

*Notwithstanding I have a few things against thee, because thou sufferest that woman Jezebel, which calleth herself a prophetess, to teach and to seduce my servants to commit fornication, and to eat things sacrificed unto idols –
Revelation 2:20*

Religious leaders and personnel have become like Ahab in the spirit, and carried Jezebel's whoredoms into the church. It (*religious idolatry*) has become the norm insomuch that it is now tolerated.

But I have this against you: that you tolerate the woman Jezebel, who calls herself a prophetess [claiming to be inspired], and who is teaching and leading astray my servants – Revelation 12:20 (Amplified Bible)

This wicked spirit must be addressed. No longer can we subscribe to and support religious 'pimps and players' in the pulpit disguising themselves as a spokesman and representatives of God.

For such are false apostles, deceitful workers, transforming themselves into the apostles of Christ. And no marvel; for Satan himself is transformed into an angel of light. Therefore it is no great thing if his ministers also be transformed as the ministers of righteousness – 2 Corinthians 11:13-15

Idolizing leaders and placing leaders on a pedestal has opened the door to a permissive spirit. This permissiveness is the penetration point of those that bring a mixture into the church. It embraces and condones evil behavior and holds no one accountable. It compromises the truth for religious prestige, power and celebrity status.

Through Jezebel's whoredoms we now have an acceptable tolerance for homosexual preachers, first gentlemen, prophetic divas and racist racketeers that sport bishop robes and drive Bentley's. Many never bat-an-eye at the surge of effeminate choir members and praise singers. Much of this is possible by believers idolizing molesting Bishops, and self proclaimed Apostles that have turned the church into a club, while hiding behind a false anointing or mission statement that speaks more about being "relevant" than "radical." The church was never commissioned to fit into a pop subculture or for than matter a religious culture. Rather it should align with a Kingdom culture that proclaims the 'Good-News' whereby the evil hearts of man can shift and as such, steer the culture towards Godly values and applications.

Leaders - Stop being an Ahab

Ahab is the permissive spirit in leaders that allows Jezebel to go buck wild and run out of control. He (the leader) is the authority figure that she gets her initial authority from.

Permissive Ahab leaders that attract Jezebel's whoredoms bring destruction to individuals, families and society at-large. The church is the bride of Christ and the bridegroom is Jesus Christ. Ahab leaders are adulterous sell-outs that destroy the purity of the church and replace it with egocentric behavior and motives.

Some leading indicators of an Ahab leader is:

- Lacks conviction
- Demands attention
- Is moody, sneaky and at times –childish
- Flatters those he/she comes in contact with
- Avoids confrontation
- Gossips and slanders about other leaders
- Willing to deceive himself
- False Repentance
- Sexually perverted and promiscuous

Congregations that have Ahab type leadership may experience:

- Increase in family break ups (divorce, separation)
- Increased lack or poverty (Financially bound)
- Guilt
- Depression
- Division & Discord
- Increase in emotional trauma
- Instability

Ahab leaders can be very gifted and out-going, but they typically lack integrity and character. They have no interest in stopping injustices or promoting truth but rather seek comfort in promoting their agenda and fitting in to the religious culture. They are quick to excuse and overlook their faults and behaviors. Ahab leaders will often take doubts and questions as a personal attack. When they're questioned, they stare at the one questioning them (or their teaching) as rebellion, stubbornness, or they will spiritualized it as a demonic scheme to undermine "God's anointed."

Ahab leaders ride on the backs of other leaders. They will use someone else's name, status, notoriety and success to elevate their own personal ministry. They can be found engaged in scandalous activities such as reality T.V. shows where they are able to poison the weak-minded. To engage in such scandal is clearly not conducive with Kingdom values or character. There is also a growing trend among these Ahab preachers where they will initiate false relationships with key influencers simply as a means of attaining their personal goals. Many come with a painted face, false humility and false covenant. They use it as camouflage to remain undetected from others, specifically the genuine sons and daughters of their intended prey.

Ahab leaders are master manipulators that strategically 'grease the palms' of those that can get them where they need to go. They will temporarily promote, travel with, or invite their "*source-daddy*" to speak in their churches simply as a political weapon to attract followers.

Once their foot is in the door and they secure the backing of the targeted leader, they use it as a channel to load their calendar full of speaking engagements, and becoming the guest preacher on as many stages as they can. As their stock increases, they slowly develop an exit strategy to disconnect from the leader that promoted them. They will transition from student/servant to Master/Elitist. They stay connected to those that are part of their manipulative conspiracy or who are able to promote them in tributaries they've yet to tap into. All others are ostracized. They have a false fathering spirit about themselves and will begin to gather many sons and daughters, promoting this illusion through photo-ops and self-proclamation. Over time they move from approachable to inaccessible. At some point they may move-on from the individual or group that they used. Many will do so abruptly. This is very strategic - as the Jezebelic spirit operating in them knows that exposure is imminent. Unfortunately those that engage in this type of activity are deceived and believe that what they are doing is right. Some will even use terms such as "*my season is up,*" or "*Gods moving me to another level.*"

This is a tragedy and is obviously part of Jezebels ever growing network in the religious culture. It is designed to pervert genuine covenant relationships and release her whoredoms. Additionally, Ahab leaders will defer responsibility and authority to the Jezebel, who is in control. This can be in the form of a network, a denomination or an overseer. In other words, whatever the Jezebelic leader or system does and says, is what the Ahab leader does.

Ahab leaders also view the church through a culture filter that is motivated through racism and tradition. Unwilling to go against the grain of the past, they quickly plug into what's familiar to them.

Kingdom truth must be preached at all cost. Fame, fortune, numbers, large buildings, fear of offending or being ostracized by ones peer, racial or economic group should not distract one from releasing the truth of God's word. Ahab leaders always support and promote the religious, traditional and racist spirit in the church. Remember:

- Religion tells you WHAT TO DO.
- Tradition tells you HOW TO DO IT.
- Racism tells you WHO CAN DO IT.

These three are the roots of deviant behavior, its influence and the conception of additional Ahab's, Jezebels and her offspring within the church.

To eradicate Jezebels and her whoredom (idolatries) from the church you must deal with Ahab first. This means leaders and those in leadership positions must be dealt with. To insure Ahab cannot return, he has to be replaced with a Jehu type leader, or leader that promotes values, morals, ethics and principles rather than their own personal self or ministry.

Jehu was a righteous man of legitimate authority and sound character that was willing to take action. Leaders that do not possess this character need to be removed from leadership. Those that follow Ahab type leaders should disconnect and follow a leader that possesses genuine leadership attributes.

I believe that God is raising up New Breed, Kingdom minded leaders and believers that will be able to discern the *"players, haters and manipulators"* in the church. These are those that will contend, challenge and expose the works of darkness.

Have nothing to do with the fruitless deeds of darkness, but rather expose them – Ephesians 5:11 (NIV)

Great leaders are leaders that serve, empower and add value to those that follow them as they follow Christ. They're leaders that will seed their potential greatness with seeds of self-sacrifice and love.

Further, these breakthrough leaders will have a strong desire for deliverance and transparency. Deliverance is the children's bread and must begin at the pulpit and with the leader. Remember, everything rises and falls on leadership. Leaders should go through deliverance. They must root out all religious demons and demonic strongholds in the mind. They must disconnect from the soul ties they have with toxic leaders, organizations or networks.

One of the things I've noticed is that both leaders and followers alike associate with those that do not pass the litmus test of being a quality Kingdom leader. Subsequently they may end up following an individual or organization that has a hidden agenda, or is not mindful of the things of God. New Breed leaders will not give attention to the things of the flesh (*self*) but rather the things of God (*Kingdom*). They will be intentional in their leadership methods and possess qualities that expand the church (not only their church) and advance the Kingdom (not their self-made kingdom). Some of those qualities are:

- Strong Convictions
- Accountability
- Responsibleness
- Commitment
- Humility
- Integrity
- Discipline
- Love

These great (*New Breed*) leaders have a servant's heart. Jesus equated servant-hood with greatness. Many lust after greatness yet will never achieve it due to their inability to serve those that have lesser status or ability. Remember if you desire to be great - you will do so by serving those you are called to lead.

Followers – Get out of Jezebel's Bedchamber

*Take note: I will throw her on a **bed** [of anguish], and those who commit adultery with her [her paramours] I will bring down to pressing distress and severe affliction, unless they turn away their minds from conduct [such as] hers and repent of their doings. And I will strike **her children** (her proper followers) dead [thoroughly exterminating them]. And all the assemblies (churches) shall recognize and understand that I am He Who searches minds (the thoughts, feelings, and purposes) and the [inmost] hearts, and I will give to each of you [the reward for what you have done] as your work deserves – Revelation 2:22-23 (Amplified Bible)*

Everyone follows someone. There is nothing wrong with following. Even leaders follow other leaders. Paul told the churches in Corinth, Philippi and Thessalonica to *"follow after him."*

However, followers cannot engage in religious idolatries by partnering with Jezebel's whoredoms. It's time for all believers to take a serious look into the Word of God and ask, "Where did the things I follow (and do) come from [and] what am I connected to?"

Similar to the children of Israel that demanded Aaron (their temporary leader) to make gods for them to follow, so have some believers today, placed a demand on preachers, churches, denominations and praise bands to make to themselves as *"entertainment gods"* so they can follow them. As Israel of Moses' day was accustomed to having visual representations of gods, some believers today desire their religious culture and iconic figureheads to be idols. Whether religious personalities, garments, artifacts, terminology, protocol, procedures, sounds or behavior; anything that draws people to a person or gathering more than it draws them to Christ - becomes an idol. Jesus said:

And I, if I be lifted up from the earth, will draw all men unto me – John 12:32

The Apostle Paul wrote to the church in Corinth,

Brothers and sisters, when I came to you, I did not come with eloquence or human wisdom as I proclaimed to you the testimony about God. For I resolved to know nothing while I was with you except Jesus Christ and him crucified. I came to you in weakness with great fear and trembling. My message and my preaching were not with wise and persuasive words, but with a demonstration of the

Spirit's power, so that your faith might not rest on human wisdom, but on God's power - 1 Corinthians 2:1-5 (NIV)

Paul was not there to put on a show. Rather, Paul stayed out of the way as much as possible. Paul did not use flamboyant techniques or gimmicks to emotionally ignite the crowd. Emotion and passion is fine, however, emotional stirrings that are created by a charismatic personality are not always the result of the Holy Spirit.
It is easy to be swayed by dynamic speakers, and preachers showboating their self-serving antics if you are seeking religion rather than the Kingdom.

But seek ye first the kingdom of God, and his righteousness; and all these things shall be added unto you.
– Matthew 6:33

The minute preaching becomes about the preacher, or ministry becomes about your ministry the anointing of the Holy Spirit is hindered regardless of how much emotion or entertainment is present on the part of the preacher and the hearers. Paul goes on to say ......

Now we have received, not the spirit of the world, but the spirit which is of God; that we might know the things that are freely given to us of God - 1 Corinthians 2:12

The spirit of this world has confidence in the flesh. The flesh is the spirit of pride, which the Word of God refers to as the pride of life. However, the World also includes religion. The scribes and Pharisees [religious leaders] of Jesus' day were of the world. They paraded around in public, seeking attention and recognition, wanting others to look up to them. They were not of the Kingdom.

*But woe unto you, scribes and Pharisees, hypocrites! for ye shut up the **kingdom** of heaven against men: for ye **neither go in yourselves**, neither suffer ye them that are entering to go in – Matthew 23:13*

Those who are of the religious-prideful spirit are part of Jezebels whoredoms. Jezebel was birthed out of religion. This spirit loves to collect flattering titles and desires others to recognize their superiority. Brothers and sisters, it's time to disconnect from the religious-idolatrous spirit that has hoodwinked the church.

I'm amazed at the number of people that contact our ministry that have been abused by the controlling Jezebel spirit (religion) operating in leaders they sit under and churches they financially support. While they desire relief from the hurt and pain associated with the abuse, many are unwilling to disconnect from it. It's very similar to a woman in an abusive relationship. She despises the pain yet will not leave.

When you realize you are in a controlling Jezebel network (church, denomination or network) or connected to an Ahab-type leader, it is best to leave. Many members remain, thinking their presence will help change the situation or person, but this is highly unlikely. In fact, remaining may perpetuate the existence of Jezebel's whoredoms. If you're in a position where you're able to contend and challenge the system or leader, and they're humble and teachable – this is the best option. Anyone that is teachable is salvageable. However the stark reality is that the religious spirit deployed by Jezebel is a tough nut to crack. Religious personnel and systems are full of pride and typically will not repent or give up their kingdom.

I gave her a chance to change her ways, but she has no intention of giving up a career in the god–business – Revelation 2:21 (Message Bible)

Have you been sleeping with the enemy? Have you been in Jezebel's bed of whoredoms? If so, stop serving Jezebel and throw her out of your life …… now! Confess your sin and ask Jesus for His forgiveness.

If we confess our sins, he is faithful and just to forgive us our sins, and to cleanse us from all unrighteousness (1 John 1:9)

Disconnect from and sever ungodly soul-ties and ungodly spiritual contracts with Jezebel and Ahab.

"What accord has Christ with Belial? Or what portion does a believer share with an unbeliever?" – 2 Corinthians 6:15 (ESV)

Finally, you must take authority over fear and false compassion. One of the things Jezebel is notorious for is intimidating those that challenge her. Remember, Queen Jezebel of old had the mighty Prophet Elijah running for his life. At one point he was so bound with depression that he wanted to die. Watch for spirits of depression and suicide when breaking from Jezebels whoredoms working through leaders. Do not fear Jezebel or Ahab. Be careful that you are not lured back into her web. Jezebel will deploy her eunuchs once you detach in hope of getting you to look back. She will make it seem as if you have lost everything. This is nothing more than a lie.

Freedom is yours - enjoy it. Spend intimate time with God. Allow the Holy Spirit to teach you the truth of the Word of God. Spend quality time in prayer and worship God in your newfound liberty. Don't be like Lot's wife:

Lot's wife <u>looked back</u> and turned into a column of salt. – Genesis 19:26 (God's Word)

Never look back at the whoredoms of Jezebel.

Section Two
Jezebels Perversions

Jezebel is a lying spirit that looks to deceive and lead many astray. Jezebel will release lies, accusations, withhold information, gossip and manufacture trouble within a church, family or business. Jezebel is a troublemaker that instigates havoc everywhere she goes. She accomplishes this by perverting every area of life. She starts by systematically and strategically cultivating a mindset that embraces dysfunction. The Jezebel spirit goes to great lengths to "normalize" dysfunction. Dysfunction occurs when we deviate from that which is normal. When we digress from what is normal, we corrupt and distort the plan, purpose and intention of God. That's perversion!

Perversion can be defined as:

1. The alteration of something from its original course, meaning, or state to a distortion or corruption of what was first intended.

    Synonyms include: distortion, misrepresentation, falsification, travesty, misinterpretation, twisting, corruption, misuse, misapplication, debasement and misconstruction.

2. Sexual behavior or desire that is considered abnormal or unacceptable.

Synonyms include: deviance, abnormality; depravity, degeneracy, debauchery, corruption, vice, wickedness, immorality.

Most people when hearing the word "perversion" immediately think in terms of sexual deviance only. While sexual perversion is found in Jezebel's cache' of weapons, it does not stop there.

Perversions start in the Mind

For the purpose of having a solid and workable definition of perversion with respect to this section, let's utilize the following:

> "The alteration of something from its original course, meaning, or state to a distortion or corruption of what was first intended."

Using this definition its clear anything can be perverted. For example using opiates for non-medicinal purposes would be a perversion of the poppy plant. Grapes and berries can be perverted into a beverage that intoxicates and causes severe health risks. The marijuana plant can be processed and used in a perverted manner causing a chemical imbalance in the brain and affecting a person's judgment or impair a persons ability to function <u>normally</u>. It can lead to poor academic performance, or for some even addiction.

Other areas that may be less obvious yet just as dangerous when it comes to being 'perverted' are:

- Perverted Purpose
- Perverted Thoughts
- Perverted Doctrine
- Perverted Relationships
- Perverted Speech
- Perverted Prophetic
- Perverted Worship
- Perverted Families
- Perverted Leaders

Let's explore each of these in a little more detail.

Perverted Purpose

This is an area that Jezebel exploits and has been highly successful in. Perverting one's purpose in life. She typically starts by inserting her deep toxic fangs of religion into a believer's life. If Jezebel can entangle you into her web of religion then she's got you.

One specific area where Jezebel has deceived believers is getting them to think that their purpose in life is going to church or being part of some religious activity center. Through religiosity she has masterfully manipulated many to spend enormous amount of time and other resources, meandering their way around various sects. Certainly, attending a quality 'Equipping Center' and assembling oneself with the body of Christ is not to be abandoned, it is not your purpose. Your purpose is not the church. <u>You are the church</u>.

And I say also unto thee, That thou art Peter, and upon this rock I will build my church; and the gates of hell shall not prevail against it – Matthew 16:18

And he is the head of the body, the church ..... – Colossians 1:18

And hath put all things under his feet, and gave him to be the head over all things to the church, Which is his body, the fulness of him that filleth all in all – Ephesians 1:22

The key to understanding purpose can be found in God's original intent. If we understand God's purposeful intent for us from the beginning then we can chart the course for where we need to be. When intent is unknown, confusion and misunderstanding is inevitable. What better environment for Jezebel to flourish in than confusion.

God's original purpose for us is unmistakably stated in the first chapter of the Book of Genesis.

And God said, Let us make man in our image, after our likeness: and let them have dominion over the fish of the sea, and over the fowl of the air, and over the cattle, and over all the earth, and over every creeping thing that creepeth upon the earth. So God created man in his own image, in the image of God created he him; male and female created he them. And God blessed them, and God said unto them, Be fruitful, and multiply, and replenish the earth, and subdue it: and have dominion over the fish of the sea, and over the fowl of the air, and over every living thing that moveth upon the earth – Genesis 1:26-28

God's purpose for mankind is:

1) Dominion – meaning to govern, manage, rule, reign, have jurisdiction and seniority over all His creation (with the exception of other people)
2) Be Fruitful – meaning you are to grow and bring increase by expanding His invisible Kingdom on Earth
3) Multiply – meaning have an abundance, excel in life, to make a heap, overflow
4) Replenish – meaning replace what is worn out, depleted or broke, restore, renew and fill up again
5) Subdue – meaning to conquer, control & dominate (with the exception of other people)

Jesus did not come to bring mankind a religion. Jesus came to restore what mankind lost.

For the Son of man is come to seek and to save that which was lost – Luke 19:10

Notice the Holy Spirit was very precise when He inspired the Scriptures. It does not say, seek and save "**those**" which are lost. – It says, "**that**" which was lost. The word save is the Greek word *'sozo'* which means to save from destruction, save something in its entirety, or to restore to completeness. It also means to deliver from the consequences of our fallen nature called **SIN** - the refusal to permit God to be God in your life.

Mankind did not lose a church, a gathering, a religion, an activity or an event. Mankind lost a Kingdom. Jesus came to bring the Kingdom back to God's delegated authorities – Man.

From that time Jesus began to preach, and to say, Repent: for the kingdom of heaven is <u>at hand</u> – Matthew 4:17

When some thing is at hand - it is right there. The phrase *'at hand'* in this verse cannot be interpreted to mean two thousand years (or longer) away. Jesus was not speaking in vague terms that no one could understand. Rather He specifically and intentionally stated that the Kingdom (which mankind lost) was being restore back to them. That was, and still is - The Good News.

Jesus accomplished His purpose. Returning that which was lost back to its original condition. He restored completely what had been lost, and when He died on the cross He cried out *"It is finished."* Jesus had accomplished the purpose He had been sent for. He had returned to its original condition everything that had been lost. He reconciled mankind back to God and He restored man's dominion over the earth.

Jezebel has perverted many minds into thinking that their purpose is church and ministry. This ideology has destroyed many marriages, families, careers, dreams and lives. Many people die never understanding their true purpose in life. Others never serve their 'gift' to the generation they were sent to serve. Still others become so successful in playing the religious game that they never succeed in God's original purpose for their life. This is a travesty in itself.

Additionally Jezebel will amplify her perversion by telling you that by gathering in a church building or at a conference that somehow you "enter into God's presence." This is another lie. God's Presence is not localized "in temples made with hands."

Howbeit the most High dwelleth not in temples made with hands – Acts 7:48

Your body is now the temple of God, and the Spirit of God dwells within you.

………… ye are God's building - 1 Corinthians 3:9

Know ye not that ye are the temple of God, and that the Spirit of God dwelleth in you? If any man defile the temple of God, him shall God destroy; for the temple of God is holy, which temple ye are - 1 Corinthians 3: 16-17

So, it's perversion to think your purpose is attending and spending enormous amount of time in religious indoctrination centers.

By now you may be wondering – "should I go and gather (assemble) at a Church?" Again, a building is not the Church – YOU ARE THE CHURCH! Also, the real question regarding gatherings is not, "Are we to gather together? " But rather, "How and why are we to gather together?"

The Apostle Paul provides us with details on 'how' we are to gather together and 'what' we're to do when we assemble as a corporate body.

*"So here's what I want you to do. When you **gather for worship**, each one of you be prepared with something that will be useful for all: Sing a hymn, teach a lesson, tell a story, lead a prayer, provide an insight. If prayers are offered in tongues, two or three's the limit, and then only if someone is present who can interpret what you're saying. Otherwise, keep it between God and yourself. And no more than two or three speakers at a meeting, with the rest of you listening and taking it to heart. Take your turn, no one*

*person taking over. Then each speaker gets a chance to say something special from God, and you all learn from each other. If you choose to speak, you're also responsible for how and when you speak. When we worship the right way, God doesn't stir us up into confusion; he brings us into harmony. This goes for all the churches—**no exceptions**" –*
I Corinthians 14:26-33 (Message Bible)

To distort this "manner" of New Testament worship gatherings opens the door to perversion. You'd have to be blind not to see this truth. In the book of Ephesians, Paul goes on to tell us that the body of Christ needs to be *"equipped"* so they can engage in the work of ministry (*serving*) and grow (*mature)* in the things of the Kingdom.

*He handed out gifts above and below, filled heaven with his gifts, filled earth with his gifts. He handed out gifts of apostle, prophet, evangelist, and pastor–teacher **to train Christians** in skilled servant work, working within Christ's body, the church, until we're all moving rhythmically and easily with each other, efficient and graceful in response to God's Son, fully mature adults, fully developed within and without, fully alive like Christ – Ephesians 4: 11-13*
(Message Bible)

As such, the primary purpose of the ascension gifts is to equip every believer, not control them.

Finally, where you gather is not the focal point. I agree that we need to have buildings, both large and small, to gather the people together so we can release doctrinal truth to the masses. That simply makes sense. Yet a gathering can occur when two or more believers come together as a body (*ref: Mat 18:20*). However, this can be in a home or the local coffee shop. The main thing is that we understand the purpose.

Once you get the revelation that your purpose is much greater than attending, gathering or being a part of a institutionalized church, I guarantee that the Jezebel spirit will lose it's hold on your life.

Remember, your purpose is found in God's original purpose (intent) for you. Stay true to God's plan and purpose and Jezebel will have no power over you.

Many are the plans in the mind of a man, but it is the <u>purpose of the Lord</u> that will stand – Proverbs 19:21 (ESV)

Perverted Thoughts

Here's another area that Jezebel releases her toxic arrows of destruction in – Thoughts. If Jezebel can corrupt your thoughts, she can control your life.

For as he thinketh in his heart, so is he - Proverbs 23:7

A perverted thought is any thought that goes contrary to the Word of God. When a believer becomes born-again their spirit gets regenerated but the Soul does not. The Soul includes the mind, will and emotions. According to Romans chapter 12, it is the responsibility of every believer to renew their mind to the will of the King. The King is Jesus and Jesus is the Word of God.

And be not conformed to this world: but be ye transformed by the renewing of your mind, that ye may prove what is that good, and acceptable, and perfect, will of God – Romans 12:2

As a believer, you have the responsibility to renew your mind. You can do this by intentionally rewiring and reprogramming your brain. This can be at the hands of powerful preaching.

So then faith cometh by hearing, and hearing by the word of God – Romans 10:17

As you continuously hear that you have been made a son of God, a joint heir with Christ and a citizen and ambassador of the Kingdom of Heaven, your thinking shifts. Once you comprehend that you have been bought at a great price, you should realize that you are highly valued. Further, you have been given a completely new nature *(2 Cor 5:17)*. This alone should cause you to think differently, thus enabling you to make better choices and decisions in your life. That's what life is about, making quality decisions.

Renewing the mind is not difficult but it takes a conscious effort on your part. You cannot have someone lay his or her hands on you to renew your mind. You cannot pray for your mind to be renewed by God. It's not His responsibility. He gave you the tools to renew your mind. He gave you His Word. Simply hear and obey His word. He also gave you a will. One of the greatest gifts God gave mankind is the freedom to choose for himself. God is not a controlling puppet-master that will make you do something. Certainly this holds true in the area of renewing your mind. It's your job – *Just Do It!*

To renew your mind you will need to study the Word of God, get equipped by the five ascension gifts describe in the forth chapter of the book of Ephesians and constantly and consistently be mindful of the Word of God. To be mindful means to be aware. Increasing your awareness of Kingdom principles will have a lasting effect on your conscious and subconscious mind. The mind is the arena where Jezebel's perversions occur.

When your mind is not on the things of God, there is no peace.

Thou wilt keep him in perfect peace, whose <u>mind</u> is stayed on thee ……… Isaiah 26:3

When you're not mindful of the things of God, you become *[like]* Satan. Jesus told Peter *[a man]* that he was Satan. The reason Jesus called Peter Satan was he *[Peter]* was not intentionally mindful of the things of God. Rather, Peter was focused on his-self.

But He turned and said to Peter, " Get behind Me, Satan! You are an offense to Me, for you are not mindful of the things of God, but the things of men – Matthew 16:23 (NKJV)

Jezebel's perversion of the mind will have you drift from the purpose and plan that God has for your life and convince you to settle on fleshly desires that yield no fruit or bring increase in your life.

Thinking negatively about oneself is perverted thinking. God wants you to think of yourself in a positive manner, regardless of actions or past behavior and experiences. Stop falling into Jezebel's trap by thinking that you're nobody. There's a religious cliché out there that many believers say. It goes like this; *"I'm just a nobody, trying to tell everybody about somebody."* Have you heard that before? Perhaps you've said it yourself. If so, renounce that alignment with Jezebel's perversion and begin to say what the Word of God says about you instead:

- I am God's child. *(Gal 3:26)*
- I am Jesus' friend (Jn 15:15)

- I am a whole new person with a completely new life *(2 Cor 5:17)*
- I am a place where God's Spirit lives *(1 Cor 6:19)*
- I am God's incredible work of art (*Eph 2:10*)
- I am totally and completely forgiven *(1 Jn 1:9)*
- I am created in God's likeness (*Eph 4:24*)
- I am spiritually alive *(Eph 2:5)*
- I am a citizen of Heaven *(Phil 3:20)*
- I am God's messenger to the world *(Acts 1:8)*
- I am God's disciple-maker *(Matt 28:19)*
- I am the salt of the earth (*Matt 5:13*)
- I am the light of the world *(Matt 5:14)*
- I am greatly loved *(Romans 5:8)*
- I am a demon buster *(Mk 16:17)*

Make these scriptural declarations daily. Personalized them just for you:

- I am crucified with Christ and I no longer live, but Christ lives in me. *(Gal 2:20)*
- The Son has set me free. Therefore I am free indeed! *(Jn 8:36)*
- My body is the temple of the Holy Spirit. *(1 Cor 6:19)*
- I can do all things through Christ who gives me strength. *(Phil 4:13)*
- There is now no condemnation (in me) because I am in Christ Jesus. *(Rom 8:1)*
- Nothing can ever separate me from the love of God in Christ Jesus. *(Rom 8:38-39)*

- In all things God works for the good of me, because I love Him. *(Rom 8:28)*
- God is faithful. He will not let me be tempted beyond what I can bear. *(1 Cor 10:13)*
- God has not given me a spirit of fear, but of power, love and a sound mind. *(2 Tim 1:7)*
- My light and momentary troubles are achieving for me an eternal glory that far outweighs them all. *(2 Cor 4:17)*
- God is able to do immeasurably more than all I ask or imagine, according to his power that is at work within me. *(Eph 3:20)*
- God is for me! Who can be against me? *(Romans 8:31)*
- I acknowledge, fully recognize and appreciate every good thing that is in me, for my identity is in Christ Jesus. *(Phm 1:6)*
- I have the mind of Christ *(1 Cor 2:16)*
- I live and have the faith of the Son of God *(Gal 2:20)*

Perverted Doctrine

*But unto you I say, and unto the rest in Thyatira, as many as have not this **doctrine**, and which have not known the depths of Satan, as they speak; I will put upon you none other burden – Revelation 2:24*

Hold on to the truth you have until I get there. Revelation 2:25 (Message Bible)

Jezebel is guilty of releasing perverted doctrine and teachings within the body of Christ. However for those that do not "have this doctrine" they are encouraged to continue to embrace the truth. An evil spirit was deceiving the church in Thyatira. That spirit was Jezebel. Today many churches are being influenced by Jezebels doctrine. We must be on guard to that which is permitted into our hearts *(minds)*.

Keep thy heart with all diligence; for out of it are the issues of life – Proverbs 4:23

Jezebel is legendary for perverting, twisting and wrangling scripture to fit her agenda. Jezebel looks for unstable souls *(minds)* that can carry her false doctrine.

…. seducing every vulnerable soul they come upon – 2 Peter 2:14 (Message Bible)

Perverted doctrine is erroneous teaching which results when individuals transform a truth from the Word of God into something entirely different than what it was originally intended to mean. The word *"perverted"* is used in the New Testament and most often means, "to turn something around and make opposite." When doctrine is perverted, it is typically turned from the manner that it was intended to mean.

There is much heresy in the church today. One of the largest heresies is the attempt to bring the church under the yoke of the Law. Religious personnel, specifically preachers, are twisting scripture in an attempt to control believers. Much of this has to do with money and numbers. They will teach on topics such as tithing by taking scripture completely out of context. I've heard preachers get on television and talk about things ranging from, "atonement seeds" to "resurrection seeds." Others have asked for offerings associated with the "feast of tabernacles" and "Passover." Perhaps they're unaware that the Old Testament and Mosaic Law is obsolete. We have a new and better covenant.

Then of course you have the "end-time madness." This is an area where doctrine as been perverted exponentially. I'm amazed at the number of believers that have been tricked in the topic of eschatology. Through twisted doctrine being pounded into their heads they have embraced a false doctrine that promotes a defeated church, a negative worldview and an escapist mentality. They have been sold a bad bill of goods when it comes to their understanding of the end of age. Yet when you exegetically explain the scriptures to them, they are so bound that they will fight you tooth and nail.

Not to be out done is the "Hyper-grace" doctrine. This twisting of doctrine is the modern sensation among evangelicals. While grace is a central theme of the Word of

God, some of these teachers have perverted it. Clearly they've gone overboard and the pendulum has swung drastically to the far left. This unbalanced teaching is sweeping churches everywhere. Whole churches and movements have oriented themselves to a distorted understanding of the gospel by espousing a 'hyper-grace.' Many of these churches and teachers refuse to take a stand against evil and rarely, if ever mention the need for repentance or deliverance.

However, this is just a small sample of the vast among of gross negligence and ignorance that exist in the lives of believers and preachers alike. An entire book could be dedicated to identify and discuss them all. Yet, I believe the two main doctrinal areas that Jezebel looks to pervert are, grace and eschatology. If you properly understand those two doctrines, religious legalism will have a difficult time controlling you.

The Apostle Paul in his letter to the in Galatia wrote;

"I marvel that ye are so soon removed from him that called you into the grace of Christ unto another gospel: Which is not another; but there be some that trouble you, and would pervert the gospel of Christ. But though we, or an angel from heaven, preach any other gospel unto you than that which we have preached unto you, let him be accursed. As we said before, so say I now again, If any man

preach any other gospel unto you than that ye have received, let him be accursed – Galatians 1:6-9"

Paul's concern was that some had entered into their company that "perverted" the gospel by teaching *"another"* message. This is a classic Jezebelic maneuver designed to entangle the saints into legalism, tradition and religious bondage. To "be accursed" means to be damned. Those who pervert the truth are in danger of damnation. God does not like perverted doctrine or those who teach it! The results are extremely debilitating for the saints that fall prey to Jezebel's perversion.

Paul goes on to say in his letter that they were being "bewitched" through the perverted teaching of religious zealots. Paul constantly dealt with false ministers (operating out of a spirit of Jezebel) who perverted the truth in order to gain control in local assemblies.

Throughout history, Israel was notorious for engaging in pagan activities and idolatry. Of course, this had much to do with Queen Jezebel's insidious plans to institutionalize witchcraft, sorcery and idolatry in Israel. Her perversion not only paved the way for pagan-god worship, but also the rise of perverted prophets and false shepherds. The prophet Jeremiah, years later, would address those that said they were speaking for the Lord but clearly were not. They perverted the word of God.

And the burden of the LORD shall ye mention no more: for every man's word shall be his burden; for ye have <u>perverted</u> the words of the living God, of the LORD of hosts our God – Jeremiah 23:36

Peter in his second letter to various churches in Asia Minor wrote:

"……… our beloved brother Paul also wrote to you according to the wisdom given him as he does in all his letters when he speaks in them of these matters. There are some things in them that are hard to understand, which the ignorant and unstable twist to their own destruction, as they do the other Scriptures" – 2 Peter 3:15-16 (English Standard Version)

Jezebel uses ignorant and unstable souls to assist in broadening her campaign to pervert and twist the scriptures. As believers and ministers of deliverance we must remain on the side of the Lord and guard against perverted doctrine of demons released by unstable preachers. Beware of fancy messages that generate a lot of excitement and shouting, yet have no depth scripturally. There are many deceived Christians today that can be found singing and praising the Lord in churches everywhere, yet they're enslaved by false doctrine. Multitudes are sitting under teachers who are perverting the Word of God. Amazingly, the majority of people come away saying, "Wasn't that powerful?"

Perverted Relationships

Merriam-Webster Dictionary defines Relationships as "a state of affairs existing between those having relations or dealings." It can be the mutual dealings, connections, or feelings that exist between two parties, countries, people, etc.

Therefore, we have relationships with anyone who we come in contact with on a regular or frequent basis. Most of these relationships are healthy, productive and bring value to all involved. Some relationships are bad, foul and perverse. These are called "perverted relationships." Again, perversion is something that is corrupt, misused, misapplied, and contaminated.

Have you ever been in a relationship with someone (or something) where you invested time, energy and resource into it, and then found out that you never were supposed to be in it in the first place? Think of all the years lost, energy expended and frustration that occurred simply due to connecting with the wrong person or thing.

God created us to have relationships with one another. Unfortunately when Jezebel is busy wrecking havoc in one's life, those relationships can become chaotic, confusing, controlling, manipulative, hostile and dysfunctional. A perverted relationship can cause you to miscarry the purpose that is to be birthed out of your life.

Jezebel infests many relationships in the 21st century. Social friendships, family and marriage relationships are all suffering as Jezebel navigates her perverted tactics strategically under the radar.

Let's look at how this works:

It all starts with the host. The host is the person (male or female) who is harboring the spirit of Jezebel. This person looks to enter into some type of relationship with you. This can be a simple friendship, business partnership, and family or marriage relationship. As the relationship progresses the Jezebelic host will begin to form a tether or soul tie with you. A soul tie is a deeply seeded bond between two souls in the spiritual realm.

Not all soul ties are perverted. For example, in a marriage relationship a "soul tie" between a husband and wife is a good thing *"if"* the marriage is properly aligned with Godly attributes and behavior. Friendships can also have good soul ties. For example in the bible, King David and Saul's son Jonathan had a good soul tie as a result of a good friendship.

And it came to pass, when he had made an end of speaking unto Saul, that the soul of Jonathan was knit with the soul of David, and Jonathan loved him as his own soul.
- 1 Samuel 18:1

However a bad soul tie can easily be formed from a corrupt relationship. Idolizing or an obsession with someone can cause an evil soul tie.

Jezebel desires to create a soul tie with you on an emotional level. Remember, Jezebel is a Narcissistic spirit that needs to maintain a consistent supply of submissive eunuchs' to do her bidding. She will utilize perverted tricks to subvert, control and undermine those she is in relationship with. One of the keys of her success is to get you to feel secure in the relationship. This "security" is a false security that has an undermining objective to ultimately get you to submit your will to her. The initial comfort you experience provides a euphoric sense of belonging. It is essentially like placing you in a room that has the ideal room temperature, relaxing Lazy-Boy© recliner, soft ambient lighting, and soothing entertainment. The only thing that you are unaware of is, the door to that room is bolted shut.

Jezebel's goal is to suck the life out of as many relationships as possible. To accomplish this she deploys multiple tactics with the purpose to mold you and get you to focus, serve and submit to her. Some of those tactics include:

Mind Games

Jezebel targets her mind games at people that are unstable. Unstable mindsets include people that are double-minded, hurt, rejected, rebellious and prideful. Jezebel creates soul ties by getting you to think that she is in your corner and has your best interest at hand. Make no mistake about it; Jezebel is a destructive spirit that leaves a long trail of damaged relationships.

Jezebel often plays mind games with those she's in a relationship with. This is often done through the push – pull tactic. She will give you attention one minute, but then to display her dominion over you she will take that attention away and shift it to another person. If you are in a perverted relationship with a person you can identify it in many cases if you are constantly on an emotional roller coaster where you feel hot one minute, and cold the next. It's basically an on and off type relationship. One day everything is good, and you feel wonderful. The next day things are not so good, and you feel sad or depressed. This is a deliberate strategy from Jezebel to entangle you in her web of destruction.

Jezebel will utilize mind games to cause you to act in a totally uncharacteristic manner. These mind games are designed to get you to think your doing something wrong. At times, you may feel as if you are losing your sanity.

Jezebel's mind tricks are designed to implement her own agenda and serve her needs.

You must be careful in establishing relationships with Jezebelic hosts. Typically you will be drawn into the relationship through false compassion by the host. Females that host the Jezebel spirit will use a "false-mothering" spirit. This spirit is designed to get you to feel as if that person sincerely cares for you. Over time, you will find yourself moving away from those that love you, are in authority and have your best interests at heart. The moment you tug away and make an attempt to get free from the controlling web, expect to be met with one of two manifestations. Either the host will lash out at you with a vengeful fury, so that you're intimidated and afraid to detach, or they will utilize pity, tears and rejection as tools of manipulation.

Gaslighting

Gaslighting is a form of emotional abuse where the abuser manipulates situations repeatedly to trick the victim into distrusting his or her own memory and perceptions. Gaslighting is an insidious form of abuse. It makes victims question the very instincts that they have counted on their whole lives, making them unsure of anything. It is the manipulation of someone through psychological means that gets them to question their own sanity. Jezebel is notorious for spinning and twisting words, situations and events. She will have you questioning your own perception of reality, even your own sanity within the established relationship. Some leading indicators that you may be in a perverted relationship is if you (are):

- Frequently second-guessing you.
- Consistently asking yourself, "Am I too sensitive or too emotional?"
- Struggling with depression when not around that person, or feel hopeless and joyless
- You feel as though you can't do anything right
- Wonder if you are a "good enough" girlfriend/boyfriend /wife/husband/ son/ daughter or friend.
- You frequently make excuses for your partner's behavior to friends and family
- You're always apologizing but really don't know why.
- You have trouble making simple decisions
- You feel confused or crazy.
- You were a very different person before you entered into this relationship.
- You know something is terribly wrong but you can never quite express what it is, even to yourself.

Additionally, here are a variety of things you may hear when engaged in a perverted relationship:

- "You're crazy – that never happened."
- "Are you sure? You tend to have a bad memory and forget things easily."

- "It's all in your head."
- "You're making this up, it never happened"
- "You're imagining things."
- "You're going to get angry over something that small?"
- "You're too sensitive, that's why nobody wants to talk to you."
- "You never believe me."
- "You have an overactive imagination."

Much of this is designed to get you to question your own motivations and perceptions rather than the issue at hand – a perverted relationship. When you start to discuss the real issues they (the Jezebel) takes a defensive posture and says things like: *"I'm not going through this again* or *"Where did you get that crazy idea?"* or *"You're always complaining and you're hurting me on purpose."*

All this is done to manipulate you (the victim) and control the relationship. This is a perverted relationship and if not addressed with Kingdom authority and dominion you are headed for a major crisis and disaster of Jezebelic proportions.

Sexual Temptation

Relationships that are not intended to be sexual or romantic need to stay platonic. However sex and sexual perversions are strategic tools used by Jezebel to pervert relationships. Many times she will use false love and compassion as a means to have you engage in sexual activities. Adding promiscuous sex, lust and perversion to a relationship does not add value to it, however a Jezebelic host will sell it as if it does.

Jezebel introduces sex into a relationship as a means of control and manipulation. She will target any opening you give her but will gravitate toward those who have been wounded by past relationships, especially family and former lovers. Some other easy prey is those that are lonely, operate out of fear of being alone, or are willing to settle for someone who lacks genuine character and godly values.

Another tactic is playing marital roles. Men and women alike must beware of this tactic. Watch for those that make statements such as, *"We love each other just as a husband and wife, so it's okay."* Of course the proverbial, *"we're going to get married anyways"*, and .... *"God understands."* All these are classic indicators of an existing perverted relationship.

When one submits to the sexual temptation, they submit to the spirit of Jezebel and create an evil (sexual) soul tie with her.

And when Shechem the son of Hamor the Hivite, prince of the country, saw her, he took her, and lay with her, and defiled her. And his soul cleaved unto Dinah the daughter of Jacob, and he loved the damsel, and spoke kindly unto the damsel." Genesis 34:2-3

Every person you have sex with leaves a part of them in you. Many victims have been traumatized, tormented, emotionally manipulated and abused by perverted relationships with men and women alike.

Have you ever had a relationship with someone and perhaps went on a few dates with him or her. Then, through whatever means, you submitted to the lure of sexual temptation and slept with them? However, deep in your heart, you knew that they were not a good match for you. But because you slept with him or her, you were not able to stay away from the relationship but kept going back. That is because Jezebel, through a perverted relationship attaches herself to you. This is a classic sexual soul tie.

Ungodly and perverted sexual relationships create ungodly soul ties to former lovers. I have ministered to many marriages and individuals that still have emotional feelings and thoughts towards ex-lovers even though they haven't seen that person in years. That person could be happily married with a family but the sexually transmitted demon is still connected to their mind. That soul tie will interfere with the genuine intimacy in the present husband-wife relationship. Thoughts of, the way it was or what that person did with you can creep into your present relationship and open the door for sexual perversions. That is a sexual soul tie.

An Ungodly Soul Tie grabs hold of you and pulls you in the past. If you find yourself unable to effectively establish relationships in your present, it could because your mind, will and emotions are still tied to a perverted relationship you had in the past. This is a very dangerous thing, and intense deliverance is necessary.

This is not unique to the traditional boyfriend/girlfriend relationship. With bombardment of liberal ideologies and an open-naked culture, the spirit of perversion has capitalized on the development of homosexual and lesbian relationships.

Remember, Jezebel is an empty vessel that wants to suck the life from you. She does this through creating Vampire-like relationships with her intended victims. Her plan and ultimate desire is to steal, kill and destroy you. It's through perverted relationships that Jezebel is able to construct a far-reaching web, which serves her purpose to maintain a constant supply of submitted subjects.

Maintaining balance

We must remember that relationships are not optional. You cannot fulfill God's call on your life without being in a relationship with Him and other people. If you've been involved in a perverted relationship repent of the damage you have caused. Further, if someone hurt you in a relationship, let it go. You must walk in forgiveness towards the one(s) that hurt you in the relationship, and pursue reconciliation with all men.

Perverted relationships with an organization

You can also have a perverted relationship with an organization. Ungodly soul ties to an organization are very common. Whether fraternities, sororities, denominational affiliations, networks or social clubs, Jezebel will use whatever tool is available to her to incapacitate you and hinder you from achieving God's plan for your life.

Ungodly soul ties can attach you to an organization through oaths and vows. These soul ties connect you to organizations that are very demonic. This can be a local church. When local churches become controlling and place heavy burdens on you that result in you feeling depressed, weary and bound, the relationship could be perverted. Be careful in signing documents of membership and affiliation to denominations. Not only is this unbiblical, but it adds absolutely no value and has no purpose other to bind the relationship to the bylaws of the organization.

Perverted Prayers

Is it possible to pray a prayer that doesn't align to the heart of God and still have it come to pass? Absolutely! We are more powerful than we think when it comes to prayer. As an ambassador from the Kingdom of God, we've been authorized by God Himself to govern the affairs of earth through our prayers. Our words have tremendous power to them when released through prayer.

Prayer is critically important in the lives of every believer. Believers are to always pray without ceasing.

Even them will I bring to my holy mountain, and make them joyful in my house of prayer: their burnt offerings and their sacrifices shall be accepted upon mine altar; for mine house shall be called an house of prayer for all people – Isaiah 56:7

However, our prayers must be governed by the word of God and the Spirit of Truth. When we pray, it's not a matter of praying what we want but rather what His will is.

Thy kingdom come. Thy will be done in earth, as it is in heaven – Matthew 6:10

Our prayers should build, edify and bring increase to self and others. They are not for the purpose of destroying lives and serving our own fleshly desires. We must be careful when we pray and not come into agreement when others pray words over us that are not in alignment with God's word. Additionally, prayers can be religious. Do you know that Jezebel loves to pray? Jezebel is a religious spirit and religious personnel 'love to pray.'

And when thou prayest, thou shalt not be as the hypocrites are: for they love to pray standing in the synagogues and in the corners of the streets, that they may be seen of men – Matthew 6:5

Many perverted prayers sound spiritual and if you are not discerning you can get caught up in the emotional drama embedded in them. This is why you must WATCH and PRAY.

Watch ye and pray, lest ye enter into temptation. The spirit truly is ready, but the flesh is weak – Mark 14:38

To watch means to give strict attention, to be cautious and active lest through some destructive calamity suddenly overtake you. Prayers motivated by the FLESH are prayers that are susceptible to Jezebel's witchcrafts.

Prayers that we ask out of our own selfishness, anger or trying to bend the will of another's are called witchcraft prayers. This is perversion.

An example of a perverted prayer would go something like this: "*Lord, if this person continue to engage in their sin, let your hand of judgment fall upon them so that they will return to you.*" Another example would be: "*Lord, I pray that you bring confusion into their home and finances until they begin to tithe and give to the church.*"

You may think that Christians don't pray such disastrous things over people's lives, but I have heard much worse. I once heard of a person that prayed for the destruction of a couple's marriage simply because the husband was married to a woman that went to a different church than they did. Obviously they prayed this prayer with sincerity and thought they were doing the will of God. But it is the spirit behind the severing of the covenant relationship *[Jezebel]*, which is orchestrating a perverted prayer, released out the mouth of an authoritative believer.

Gossip

Watch out for prayers that slander people during the actual prayer process. Prayers that slander an individual's character must immediately be rebuked. An example of a gossip-laced prayer would be, "*let's pray for sister Susan because y'all know she keeps getting pregnant out of wedlock*". To actually engage in that prayer would certainly be a prayer of witchcraft, sorcery and perversion.

One of the thing that creates the environment of perverted prayers in prayer teams and prayer groups are the vast amount of time spent talking versus praying. I have personally witnessed the spirit of Jezebel in operation within intercessory prayer groups. These intercessory prayer covens love to gossip about leadership or those that are not part of their "circle." They have very little intention of actually praying for the church and its leadership team. Rather, the Jezebel spirit uses the prayer team as a sounding board to tear down and destroy other ministries and individuals.

Our speech should never curse any one or anything. We are to speak life, not death.

The mouth of a righteous man is a well of life: but violence covereth the mouth of the wicked – Proverbs 10:11

………… "bless, and curse not"- Romans 12:14

Perverted Prophetic

Jezebel loves the prophetic and calls herself a prophet.

"………… Jezebel, which calleth herself a prophetess" – Revelation 2:20

I love the prophetic dimension of the church. As an Apostle of the Lord myself, I recognized the value of genuine New Testament prophetic operations and the need for the ascension gift of the Prophet to be functional in the 21st century church. Unfortunately we have tolerated the Jezebel spirit within the prophetic dimension and things have spiraled out of control. Many "so-called" Prophets and prophetic operations are nothing less than modern day prophetic spiritualists and divination. Warning - Jezebel has high-jacked the prophetic.

It's understandable how this has happened. Many years of ignorance and misapplication of sound doctrine clearly has been the largest enabler of prophetic spiritualists gaining a foothold in the church. Understandably, people today are looking for answers, instruction and direction. There is so much pain in people's lives that many have become hopeless, desperate and spiritually parched. Religiously dead churches and leaders bound by ridged and controlling by-laws or board of elders offer no solution nor do they extend any comfort. This is where genuine prophetic ministry can be like a geyser of refreshing water to a scorched and dry soul.

As the prophets and prophetic gift began to emerge in our churches, it released a much needed refreshing and revival to the body of Christ. Many years of stale, lethargic and dead moves were quickly overcome by the dynamics of the prophetic anointing moving in and on people's lives.

Prophets began to announce the re-arrival of the Apostles in the 21st Century and the reestablishment of "Antioch" modeled ministries, that equip the saints rather than endorse seeker friendly, cookie-cutter modeled ministry, that grow numerically, yet never develop the lives of the people. However, with this re-emerging came persecution. Pastors, Bishops and other religious personnel became agitated and felt threatened by this new wave of spiritual liberty that had people wanting to know more about the gift. Unfortunately, some spoke out against the Prophets, driving many of them into isolation in an attempt to quarantine them and maintain control over their ministries and the people that followed them. This was a challenge for the Prophets as well as the people. The Prophets had nowhere to turn to assist them grow and mature in their gifting.

Although rejected, many were undaunted and continued to operate in a graceful and humble manner. Unfortunately others succumbed to rejection and a sprit of pride and rebellion quickly began to hinder the genuine moves of the Holy Spirit. Rebellion is the sin of witchcraft and the spirit of Jezebel quickly capitalized on this open door. When believers walk in the flesh yet are determined to flow in the Spirit, it's a recipe for disaster.

The flesh always opens the door to witchcraft.

This I say then, Walk in the Spirit, and ye shall not fulfil the lust of the flesh – Galatians 5:16

When you follow the desires of your sinful nature, the results are very clear: sexual immorality, impurity, lustful pleasures, idolatry, sorcery (Witchcraft*), hostility, quarreling, jealousy, outbursts of anger, selfish ambition, dissension, division, envy, drunkenness, wild parties, and other sins like these. Let me tell you again, as I have before, that anyone living that sort of life will not inherit the Kingdom of God – Galatians 5: 19-21 (New Living Translation) (*insert the author)

When individuals are lead by the flesh, *(the desires of the old sinful nature)* there is a propensity to be seduced and deceived by the Jezebel spirit. Jezebel will pervert prophetic operations by implementing controlling tactics (specifically manipulation). Many will begin to release curses, judgments and false words designed to hinder the saints from entering into their true destiny. Prophecy is never to be used to judge, condemn and scorn people but rather to edify, comfort and exhort. When you see the former being done, that's perverted prophetic and you better watch out.

Additionally, Jezebel will pervert those releasing this witchcraft into seeking monetary gain and therefore have become nothing short of being a merchandiser pimping the prophetic gift or worse yet, the functional gift of the Prophet.

The Apostle Peter gave us stern warnings about this in his day when he wrote to the 1st century believers about false Prophets invading the church.

And through covetousness shall they with feigned words make merchandise of you – 2 Peter 2:3

The term *"feigned words"* is speaking about forming exaggerated sayings that are filled with lies. Prophetic operations become perverted when Jezebels prophets release outrageous words telling people to engage in behaviors that are contrary to the word of God. In one example a Prophet told a person that if they sowed a large sum of money into their ministry that the Lord would open up opportunities for them to start their business. That's perversion.

Unfortunately today there is a growing trend among prophetic circles that have the mindset that charging or being compensated for giving a prophetic word to someone is acceptable behavior. This is a perverted mindset that is instigated by the spirit of Jezebel. It is nothing more than an attempt to discredit the gifts of the Holy Spirit by aligning the prophetic with that of psychic mysticism and commerce.

I know of Prophets that operate out of a Jezebel spirit. They're easy to spot. They mostly have the same characteristics about themselves. Some things to watch out for are:

- The focus is on them.
- The focus is on *"their"* gift and they use it for *"self advancement."*
- They have no comprehension of the Kingdom.
- The Kingdom is not their priority.
- They're religious in nature.
- They teach and preach esoteric messages.
- Most of their preaching is from the Old Testament (*specifically prophetic operations*).
- They excessively use the term, *"God said,"* and *"I know this by the spirit"*.
- They are flamboyant and polished showmen who draw attention to themselves.

Because the focus is on themselves and their gift, they rarely talk about the Holy Spirit. Rather they create an illusion that they hear from God. When challenged or confronted about their erroneous ways they are quick to say, *"touch not my anointed and do my Prophets no harm."* They will not submit to the authority or others and ferociously assault their challengers, even demonizing them in an attempt to discredit the challenge. They are accountable to no one.

> "………and despise government. Presumptuous are they, selfwilled, they are not afraid to speak evil of dignities
> 2 Peter 2:10 (b)

Others have operated out of their own desires (*the flesh*) when ministering prophetically, but in reality they're tapping into the realm of the dark underworld. Those that prophesy in a perverted manner also engage in sexual uncleanliness.

> *But chiefly them that walk after the flesh in the lust of uncleanness – 2 Peter 2:10*

This perversion doesn't happen over night, but rather occurs over a sustained period of time. When people become mesmerized through the accuracy of these spiritualists, they quickly become targets for Jezebels sexual and scandalous perversions. Jezebel will always look for unstable souls. Those whom have very little to no spiritual foundation to stand on their own are prime candidates for Jezebels Prophets to develop perverted and "sexual soul ties" with.

> *Having eyes full of adultery, and that cannot cease from sin; beguiling unstable souls – 2 Peter 2:14*

Their basic mode of operation is to flatter the person receiving the smooth prophetic word into thinking that they can go to a higher level spiritually by "sleeping" with them.

What's happening to the prophetic ministry in our churches?

Much of this perversion is caused by inaccurate teaching pertaining to prophetic operations, specifically the office if the Prophet. Many teach, or have been taught from an Old Testament dimension and place more value on the gift than the Word of God and the Holy Spirit. Additionally, because the majority of churches do not "disciple" people and create a culture whereby people are dependent on the Holy Spirit, they de facto create a system that has people dependent on the "gifted" person. This is very dangerous.

Further, many spiritualists are capable of "reading one's mail." I've seen Prophets call individuals out at large gatherings and tell them their name, address and zip code. Because of the accuracy, many gravitate to these meetings, seeking additional words and direction. It has opened a portal of witchcraft and perversion that churches and ministers today build on simply to generate large crowds and notoriety. Today we have a coven of witches and warlocks that travel under the banner of the prophetic, and use the self-proclaimed title of Prophet.

The tremendous nonexistence of accountability and governing of the person operating in the gift perpetuates the problem. No one has the boldness to speak out. Even legitimate and genuine Prophets are silent for fear of being attacked from other religious leaders that support this nonsense. There is much witchcraft operating through what some call the Prophetic. Much of this is tolerated because the religious spirit muzzles the saints by twisting scriptures, leaving them fearful to address it.

The 21st century church is no different than the 1st century church in Thyatira in that they "permitted that woman—Jezebel who calls herself a prophet—to lead God's servants astray."

Certainly we should not despise prophecy, but we MOST certainly should judge it.

> *Beloved, believe not every spirit, but try the spirits whether they are of God: because many false prophets are gone out into the world – 1 John 4:1*

Believers must guard their heart from PERVERTED PROPHECY. Again, perversion is something that is corrupt, misused, misapplied, and contaminated. Some who are untrained or are not held accountable to someone of outstanding character are prancing around beguiling unstable souls through their sorcery. Therefore it is imperative that we consistently ask, *"Did the Spirit of God say that, or some other spirit?"*

The reason many prophets are operating out of another spirit or their flesh rather than the Spirit of God, is because we are not weighing, examining and placing those words on trial. Be not deceived, God is not the sender of everyone who parades around saying they're God's voice piece. We must judge prophecy by examining the "spirit' behind the words being spoken. We see this in the word of God where people spoke out of a familiar spirit.

And it came to pass, as we went to prayer, a certain damsel possessed with a spirit of divination met us, which brought her masters much gain by soothsaying: The same followed Paul and us, and cried, saying, These men are the servants of the most high God, which shew unto us the way of salvation. And this did she many days. But Paul, being grieved, turned and said to the spirit, I command thee in the name of Jesus Christ to come out of her. And he came out the same hour – Acts 16:16-18

In the above scripture we have a woman who was speaking forth words that were true, yet Paul said she had a *"spirit of divination."* Paul discerned that the woman was operating out of a spirit of flattery and did so for several days. If Paul had not addressed this issue publicly, the sorcerer would have gained credibility among the people. In another example, Jesus had to rebuke his disciples for wanting to do what Elijah did in the Old Testament; yet Jesus said they were not operating out of the Spirit of God.

And when his disciples James and John saw this, they said, Lord, wilt thou that we command fire to come down from heaven, and consume them, even as Elias did? But he turned, and rebuked them, and said, Ye know not what manner of spirit ye are of. – Luke 9:54-55

Prophesying (predicting) doom, gloom, curses and judgment on individuals and nations is not the pattern of the New Testament prophet or believer.

Let the prophets speak two or three, and let the other judge. – I Corinthians 14: 29

When is the last time you actually witnessed prophets or prophetic words judged by others? Think about it. This biblical practice has for the most part remained obsolete in our gatherings.

We must learn to reject prophecies yet we must do so without killing the prophet or discouraging the charismata from operating in our meetings. However, to idly sit back and permit Jezebel to pervert the prophetic gift is to invite witchcraft into the church. We will talk more about witchcraft in the next chapter.

Finally, the greatest enabler to the Jezebelic perversion operating in the prophetic is due to the saints feeding their flesh with more flesh. The bottom line is, many actually enjoy this perverted prophetic culture that is nothing more than divination. Many know it's wrong but they can't shake loose from the soul tie they have created with Jezebel and her prophets. Numerous people are bound by years of religion, tradition and racism that exists in churches, denominations and networks, and have grown accustom to accepting the religious culture as the norm. As such, some have glorified these "*gifted people*" and rallied around them as champions in the faith. Still others are petrified to speak out against it lest they be labeled an "outsider" or slandered against. Unable to withstand the persecution that comes when standing up for righteousness and truth, they succumb to the idolatry of their hearts and desires of the flesh, gravitating to those who tell them what they want to hear.

> *For the time will come when they will not endure sound doctrine; but after their own lusts shall they heap to themselves teachers, <u>having itching ears</u>; And they shall turn away their ears from the truth, and shall be turned unto <u>fables</u> – 2 Timothy 4:3*

A fable is a story. Beware when a Prophet isolates you and delivers private words designed to mesmerize you with their "deep spiritual" sayings. They look for "unstable souls" and know how to feed fleshly lust for power, fame, future and greatness. They will tell you precisely what your flesh wants to hear.

> *'This is what the Sovereign Lord says: The people of Israel have set up idols in their hearts and fallen into sin, and then they go to a prophet asking for a message. So I,*

the Lord, will give them the kind of answer their great idolatry deserves" – Ezekiel 14:4 *(New Living Translation)*

Indeed, this is what happened to Ahab the enabler. King Ahab employed Jezebels prophets and when Ahab and Jehoshaphat (King of Judah) inquired of them about going to war, over 400 prophets prophesied out of perversion according to Ahab's idolatry in his heart. *(ref I Kings 22)*

When your heart is not right you will attract and be lured to the spirit of perversion operating in Jezebel's prophetic counterfeit Prophets.

Perverted Worship

One of the vital things that the spirit of Jezebel will seek to destroy is the liberty, spontaneity and pureness that exist in worship vis-à-vis through the leading of the Holy Spirit.

The local church was never designed to be the place where one gets their praise on or worships the Lord.

Think about it. There is no commandment in scripture, which says that a believer must attend a church building in order to worship God. Does this statement surprise or offend you? If so, it's because the religious spirit that has invaded the church, under the direction of the Jezebel spirit, has tricked you in to thinking that you're supposed to attend *"worship services."* While there certainly is nothing wrong with worshipping and singing praise to our Lord during our gatherings, it has polarized our times together and eliminated many other things we are to do when we gather together. Paul talks specifically to the 1st Century believers in Corinth and tells them what they're to do when they gather together for worship. He tells the believers, not a team of professional "artists" to be prepared to bring something that will be useful to everyone in attendance. Such as, tell a story *(testimony)*, deliver a teaching, give a prayer, prophesy or give insight into the things of God. This is a far cry from our gatherings and worship services we have today. Quite frankly, in many of our gatherings if you were to do that, you may find yourself being rebuked and told to be quiet. You would be classified as being "out of order."

If you search the New Testament scriptures there are generally no examples of any follower of Christ going to a church building to worship God. They worshipped God by their obedience to Him in every area of life, every day of their lives. They did not worship Him by giving Him only one hour of their time every week in some temple made with hands. Rather, they were free to express their worship to God through acts of service, reading of doctrine, communing with each other and being obedient to actually living the Kingdom life.

Worship is much more than standing on your feet for thirty minutes; while someone or some praise team feverishly attempts to lead you to a place your heart may not be willing to go. No, worship is an act of expressing your love for Him and compliance to His Kingdom rule and order in your life. The Kingdom is not about a fleshly emotional release; it's about righteousness, peace and joy in the Holy Ghost. It's only in the Holy Spirit that you will find genuine worship.

Anytime we enter an environment that says this is how it's done, we create a monument of idolatry. That's tradition and legalism. In the book of John, Jesus spoke to the Samaritan woman about this very thing. She confronted Jesus on how and where to worship. Jesus responded by saying;

"Believe me, woman, the time is coming when you Samaritans will worship the Father neither here at this mountain nor there in Jerusalem." Jesus went on the say; *"But the time is coming - it has, in fact, come - when what you're called will not matter and where you go to worship will not matter."* (ref John 4:21,23 Message Bible)

Surely, Jezebel has perverted worship and in many cases has reduced it to nothing more than fleshly entertainment.

Here's another question to ask, can you worship God alone or do you need to be around others to actually engage in it? Do you have to have a certain "atmosphere" to worship or can you worship when the exterior setting is not conducive to your way of doing it?

Every believer should worship God in the beauty of His holiness and not in a pre-formatted, Jezebelic inspired patterned designed to control the worshipper. We should adore Him, worship Him, magnify Him, and honor Him and not get caught in the incapacitating web that limits the effectiveness of genuine worship. No longer can you afford to be bound to a systematically incubated structure that reduces worship to a place or specific method. This idea that the church is a place to worship God came from Rome, not from the New Testament. There is only one place in the New Testament where the word worship is connected to a public service, and that was dealing with the worshipping of false gods (*see Acts 17: 22-25*)

The only example we see in the entire New Testament of a Christian worship service is found in *1st Corinthians 14:26-33,* and the manner by which they gathered was drastically different from our current model.

In *Amos 5:21-23*, God told the people; *"I hate, I despise your feast days, and I will not smell in your solemn assemblies.... I will not accept them.... Take thou away from me the noise of thy songs...."*

The church was not made to be a <u>place</u> of organized worship. Rather it was made to be a living organism that goes out into the world and makes Kingdom disciples of all races, teaching them to obey what Jesus commanded us to do. (*Matthew 28: 19-20*)

Worship is perverted when it is prefabricated. When it's bound to a time, a day or place. Worship is everywhere. You worship on the job, in the car, in the boardroom and in the bedroom (marital covenant only please). You worship in managing the resources God has entrusted you with. That's right, being a good steward over God's property is a form of worship. How you handle yourself in life, your character and manage your time, is all worship. Worship never ceases. It's perpetual and highly fluid. Once you understand this, Jezebel will lose her religious, traditional and racists grip on your life.

There's nothing wrong with singing, dancing, waving flags, banners and blowing the shofar. I enjoy doing all that and encourage others to engage in that also. However, I have learned that if we box God in to a specific method, sound or look, we partner with Jezebel's controlling strategy to alter (pervert) the true meaning or worship.

Perverted Families

One of the main areas Jezebel looks to pervert is within the family structure. God is a God of order and intent.

When families deviate from God's original plan He has for husbands, wives and children, it is perverted. Today we have families that are missing Fathers as the leaders of our homes. The vast amount of children being born out of wedlock, to multiple *"babies mamma and daddies,"* and those who "play married" yet never make a legal covenant commitment before God and Man is a clear indication of the existence of Jezebels perverted stronghold in the family unit. The spirit of Jezebel perverts the family wherever God's divine order of authority is either not known or is ignored. God's divine order for the family is simple:

But I want you to understand that the head of every man is Christ, the head of a wife is her husband, and the head of Christ is God. 1 Corinthians 11:3 (ESV)

Jezebel hates men and is adamant about destroying them. Jezebel looks to emasculate men spiritually and emotionally. She does so by flipping the script and having women raise children independent of men. Many women in are churches today have numerous children with no Father present. Jezebel has turned men into nothing more than "studs" that sire offspring yet have no active involvement in their life.

Any time we tamper with God's structuring of family authority, values and definition it will open the woman, her children and society to satanic attack.

Christian families are now entertaining thoughts of homosexuality, lesbianism and promiscuity as being acceptable behavior and the social norm. Pastors and leaders are caving into the secular - political correct definition what constitutes a "marriage." The biblical definition of marriage is found in the word of God; "a covenant relationship between one man and one woman." In genesis chapter 2, God provides is with the standard by which all marriages are defined:

"Therefore a man shall leave his father and his mother and shall become united and cleave to his wife, and they shall become one flesh" Genesis 2:24 (Amplified Version)

Yet today we have Christian leaders condoning a position that clearly goes against our Christian faith. Many are now performing same-sex marriages. There are also cases of male Bishops marrying other men and using terms such as "first gentleman" for the same-sex partner. This is another type of perverted family. Again, perversion is defined as *"the alteration of something from its original course, meaning, or state to a distortion or corruption of what was first intended."*

Divorce

Divorce has infiltrated the church. And while some indiscriminately throw out statistics that has divorce among those who profess to be believers in the Christian faith equal to or exceeding that of their secular counterparts, there seems to be no reputable study to warrant that particular narrative. Not withstanding, a simple sampling among believers does reflect that marriages ending in divorce are much more than we should have. And while some divorcees had legitimate reasons for terminating the relationship, others simply use it as an opportunity to remedy a problem they are unwilling to work to fix. However, regardless of why one got a divorce, it's clear that we have a problem with our philosophical view on why one should get married.

Marriage is not a quick fix to satisfy one's selfishness. It should never be used as a patch to cover for one's insecurity and loneliness. Nor is it a remedy to various *"daddy issues"* one had growing up. Some women have married men to compensate for the rejection they experienced from their biological Father who abandoned them at young age. Some men have gotten married out of the need to replace their biological mother. Yet others marry to satisfy the sexual cravings of their flesh, even to the point of using scripture to defend their basis in doing so. (i.e. *"better to marry than burn with lust"*) Others marry solely on the basis of mere physical attraction. This is not only a foolish mistake but also childish. Additionally, marriage should not be entered just to cover for a child conceived out of lust and promiscuity. Marriage should never be viewed as a quick-fix formula for anything. Finally, women should not get married for the purpose of having the husband as the "high-priest" over the woman. This is erroneous teaching based on improper interpretation and twisting of the word of God.

Marriage is a picture of the magnificent relationship between Christ and His covenant people. Marriage portrays the beauty and the truth of the eternal relationship we have with God. It is a true blessing from God. The Apostle Paul wrote to the Ephesian church that marriage was a representation of Christ and His church. The husband depicts a servant leader, laying down his life within the marriage relationship as Christ does for His bride, the church. The wife follows her husband's lead, submitting to his leadership out of her own free will. This represents the Body of Christ's response to the Head of the Church, Jesus Christ.

The Jezebel spirit is dedicated to destroying the marriage relationship. She will do this initially by getting couples to marry for many of the wrong reasons listed above. She will also target the husband and lure him to abandon the marriage vow. Jezebel will use sexual temptation as a means to sever the marriage covenant. Lascivious women prancing around as sympathizers seduce many men into perversion, breaking up marriages in the process. Men must seek first the Kingdom and His righteousness, (governing rule over his life) and not yield to the temptation to being a victim of Jezebel's attacks. We need strong Christian men that place God, and His word in the heart of the marriage.

Controlling mothers (and parents)

Let me start by saying that Jezebel is not unique to females only. Jezebel is a spirit and as such, is gender-neutral. We refer to Jezebel as a "she" simply due to the fact that this spirit operated in an actual queen that lived thousands of years ago. Her name of course was Jezebel. However this spirit operates in both males and females, although women appear to be more susceptible to her attacks and potentially used as a host. Men on the other hand, appear to be targeted by Jezebels attacks then actually host this spirit themselves, although they certainly can. Needless to say, men have their own problems in contending with the Ahab spirit. This is not to be taken lightly as the Jezebel spirit operates most efficiently when working with an Ahab dominated male. Regardless, Jezebel's masquerade of trickery, sorcery and seduction targets a vast array of people and does so indiscriminately.

Jezebel will target women that have been hurt and abused to get them to carry out her assignments to pervert families. I've witness many accounts of mothers that control their sons and daughters well into their adult lives. We see this most in homes that were lead by women that were abandoned by the male figure. Whether a former lover, husband or their own biological father, the unhealed wound becomes a sore spot when in comes to men in general. Further exacerbating this problem is when they over compensate in an attempt to protect their children. A woman can become "anti-male" and indoctrinate their children with a negative view of men.

Jezebel will employee demons of retaliation that have easy access to mothers holding on to past hurt, shame, pain anger and hatred which can drive the person to a place where Jezebel can release a fury of vengeance against the mothers own children.

Perversion, control and manipulation can manifest through statements such as; *"After all I've done and sacrificed for you"* or *"This is the thanks I get"* or *"How could you do this to me?"* or *"You should be ashamed of yourself"* and finally, *"How could you even think such a thing?"* Of course this is classic Jezebel hurling accusations, blame, condemnation and guilt with the intention of controlling the relationship.

When parents feel that if they help out their grown children, that it somehow obligates the child to them – it's perversion. Such help is not done out of love, but rather for an ulterior motive - to allow the Jezebel parent to remain in a controlling position. A parent that is insistent about their child accepting their help, whether he or she asked for it or not, is operating as an aggressive Jezebel. Remember, Jezebel is a narcissist that desires to control every relationship, even that of their adult-children. Her goal is to eliminate the grown child's ability to refuse the help. Once the adult-child accepts the help, the trap is set and the many strings that are attached to the favor become the tool of this demonic puppet master. Through this deception, the adult-child's freedom of choice and right to live independently is removed.

This plays nicely into Jezebels goal of maintaining a consistent supply of victims. When the adult-child accepts the help of a Jezebelic mother, it substantiates in the host mind what they have thought about the adult-child all along- that you can't really make it without them. In their minds, if you need (and accept) help from them, you are still dependent on them. They will never see the grown child as an independent adult.

This is not to detract from parents providing relief or assistance in times of crisis and hardship to their children. Clearly, every parent should help out their children when they can. The main thing to discern is what is the motivation behind it. Many times we can do things that look good but are done out of the wrong spirit. When mothers (or fathers) help out and then feel they have the "right to protect their investment" in you by prying, making demands, or being controlling it is perversion.

Perversion occurs when mothers control their daughters (or sons) behaviors even to the point to demanding they that carry out actions against others in a manner that they deem fit. This is especially true in marriages when the mother tells a daughter (or son) what to say and do with the spouse. Mothers should not control their adult child in any manner, specifically their relationships with others. Mother should not control or manipulate how their married children raise their child either. This statement holds true for fathers as well.

Another area we see this perversion is in the mother-son relationship. Controlling mothers bound by Jezebel consistently "baby" their male adult children, even to the point of caring for them as if they were young boys. This is all part of Jezebel's attempt to "castrate" the male by having the mother rule over him, when he (the male) himself should be ruling his own life and family.

As for my people, children are their oppressors, and women rule over them. O my people, they which lead thee cause thee to err, and destroy the way of thy paths.
Isaiah 3:12

Watch for mothers that do not permit male-adult children to mature into independent men. Mothers that continue to care for their grown sons well into their twenties, thirties and beyond is dysfunctional at best. Mothers that demand an allegiance to them by the sons, creates friction in the home and humiliates the man. Many men have given up being the provider, caretaker and leader in their own homes, due to the Jezebelic pattern in the mother. The spirit of Jezebel is a militant spirit that seeks to destroy the functionality of the family to ensure that her children will not be able to operate independent of her. Many mothers have created evil soul ties with their male-children out of fear of losing them. This comes from the mother's inability to get delivered from her own rejection and abandonment.

Another area to watch out for is the grandchild. Many grandparents think that babysitting their grandchildren automatically gives them the right to interfere in the grandchildren's upbringing. Again, "helping" with the grandkids is a wonderful thing, yet it cannot come with "strings" attached or expectation of some sort of "payback." Some grandparents think that helping out with the grandkids entitles them to a say in who their adult-child dates, marries, or where they live. This is perversion as is detracts from and undermines the authority for the grandchild's parent(s).

Jezebelic mothers typically manifest in one of two types of behavior. The first is a high-profile type mother that is largely sociable, opinionated and highly visible. She is often seen as the "woman who wears the pants in the family." The second type is a mother that is soft-spoken, motherly, and protective, even gives the outward appearance of being godly and very docile. This is by far the most dangerous type and most difficult to detect. This type is capable of manipulating her children through dramatic performances that gets her children to feel sorry for her out of the guilt she casts on them. Male children are prime targets and fall prey to this seduction and perversion. Jezebelic mothers use their children as weapons to advance their self-seeking needs. Children are simply pawns in her power and control games.

Parents must validate and embrace the value of their children when growing up. If they do not, they themselves open the door for disobedience, rebellion and perversion to enter and subsequently manifest in their own children.

Disobedient and rebellious children

Families that veer away from the governing order and principles of the Kingdom of God are dysfunctional families. A byproduct of dysfunctional parents *(leaders)* is disobedient children. Today we have a disobedient society that is demonstrating the dysfunction that is operating in homes.

Jezebel in children will show up as rebellion, lying and disrespect. This is perversion. However, adult children that manipulate their parents to care for them, or place heavy burdens on them that steal from the parents right to live and enjoy life are perverting the natural child-parent relationship.

An example of this is adult children that cast their misfortunes and problems on their parents by releasing a spirit of guilt on them. If you've ever been the victim of an adult-child saying *"you brought me into this world,"* you understand what I'm saying. It is not the parent's responsibility to field all of their adult-children's responsibilities. I see this often with daughters that had children themselves at a very young age and were engrossed in toxic relationships. It's as if the mother feels responsible to fix the problem. It's very dangerous and can cause the mother to take on the "fixer-spirit."

Bullying by Adult-Children

Disobedient children can grow up into becoming full-blown adult bullies in the spirit. Spiritual bullies are those that manipulate in various areas of life, and put great burdens on parents. Essentially they plot and scheme, utilizing Jezebelic tactics to beat their parents into submission. These adult bullies are toxic predators that blame you for everything that is wrong in their life. Nothing you did in their early childhood developmental or adolescent years was good enough. They have a nasty mindset that expects more. The more you give, the more they look to take from you. It's almost as if you need to pay restitution to them for their perceived miserable life. But I must warn you, no matter what you give or say, it will never suffice the perverse - bullying spirit.

A leech has twin daughters named "Gimme" and "Gimme more" – Proverbs 30:15 (The Message Bible)

This Jezebelic bullying spirit operating in adult-children will use guilt as their primary manipulative weapon. You see; it's not necessarily that you were a bad parent, although Jezebel would have you to think that. Certainly you, like every other parent, made some mistakes. There's no user manual that's handed out when children are born. We simply do the best we can, pulling from our past on how we were raised and praying for wisdom. But we're not perfect, and Jezebel will certainly let you know that. Have you ever had a situation where a seemingly good visit or phone call with your adult child ultimately explodes into a full blown verbal or physical attack against you? You feel no matter what you do, "you're damned of you do, or damned if you don't." With these adult bullies what you do is never good enough for them.

Controlling bullies will extort you out of your money and time. They will utilize your grandchildren as pawns simply to get their way. If you want to see your grandchildren, it's as if you have to pay a bribe in order to spend time with them.

On the outside these toxic predators masquerade around as if they are wonderful children. They pretend to have a great relationship with you. This is done by design in order to create the illusion to others that they are the innocent and loving child. However in private, the bullying never ceases. As a parent you are made to feel as if you are walking on eggshells and therefore should only say that which is in agreement with the perverted mindset of the adult-child. Again this is an intimidating tactic designed to beat you into submission. Children should never abuse parents – ever!

Jezebel works through adult-children to suck from parents. She will deplete them of their energy, time and resources. She uses her unscrupulous tactics to wear resistance down in order to have you cave into her demands. If you've ever had your grown adult-children make you feel as if it's your responsibility to fix their problem after they talked to you, then Jezebel is in operation.

Ahab Fathers

Ahab fathers can place curses on male children just as Jezebel mothers place it on female children. This is why we must focus on building strong marriages and families. Fathers can cause their children to become angry and resentful by not owning up to their responsibilities as the leader of the home.

And, ye fathers, provoke not your children to wrath: but bring them up in the nurture and admonition of the Lord –
Ephesians 6:4

Fathers must be in the home, spend time with their children and understand that it is their job to raise those children correctly. They cannot continue to have a passive attitude to raising children by placing that responsibility solely on the wife (woman). Additionally, fathers must go beyond simply being in the home. Today we have fathers that while physically present; spend no time bonding with their children. Rather, they sit selfishly in their "man-cave" watching sporting events and other time-wasting programs. Fathers must be active. Further, fathers can promote hostility in their children by being critical. Criticism is always negative and harmful. When one is criticized it never brings about a positive emotional response. Critical fathers need deliverance and must to embrace the nurturing component of fathering, lest Satan gain the advantage over them and their children.

Male children can veer towards homosexual behavior, become effeminate and lethargic; the female children – lesbians, angry and promiscuous when the Father compromises his duties. These children may end up repeating the dysfunction by having broken marriages and families themselves. Jezebel mothers and Ahab Fathers cause their children to be manipulative and disobedient. Inwardly these children are full of rebellion and under satanic pressure to prove that their parents, specifically their mother was wrong in how they were raised. Therefore they end up retaliating against their parents through acts of disobedience.

For people will love only themselves and their money. They will be boastful and proud, scoffing at God, <u>disobedient to their parents</u>, and ungrateful. They will consider nothing sacred. They will be unloving and unforgiving; they will slander others and have no self-control. They will be cruel and hate what is good. They will betray their friends, be reckless, be puffed up with pride, and love pleasure rather than God. They will act religious, but they will reject the power that could make them godly. Stay away from people like that – 2 Timothy 3:2-5 (New Living Translation)

Children can be so angry that they become ungrateful, unloving and unforgiving towards their parents, specifically their father. Their mindset is that of a victim. They feel as that they were "cheated" out of a normal life and now have an "entitled right" to use and abuse their elderly parents. This is perversion.

Murmuring, complaining, criticism and blame is a type of spirit very common among Jezebelic children. Many adult-children use criticism of parental faults to build up their own self-esteem, and to justify their disobedience of, or lack of respect towards parents. There is no excuse for acting out of disobedience, fits or rage and retaliation in order to "get even." Adult children must forgive parents that succumbed to Jezebelic perversion by raising them in a dysfunctional manner. Un-forgiveness by adult children only elevates the level of bondage that they currently have. Un-forgiveness and disobedience hurts the disobedient and un-forgiving more than the one they are un-forgiving and disobedient towards.

Colossians 3:6 says that, ... *"the wrath of God [comes] upon the children of disobedience."*

It is the responsibility of both parents to bring their children up in the ways of the Lord and in an environment of love where they are developed and corrected in the love of Christ. This must start early in the childhood development years. When this process breaks down, it opens the door for Jezebel to institute her perversions and tarnish the natural progression of the child to mature adult. However, this cannot be used as a crutch to maintain a dependence on parents. Critical to everyone achieving their destiny in life is the ability to go through deliverance ministry and ultimately renew their minds.

Finally, when adult-aged children move back home with their parents it may cause some financial and emotional strain for aging parents. While there is certainly nothing wrong with helping adult-children get back on their feet in times of crisis, it is important for the parents to protect their own financial future and marriage. To place children ahead of the marriage covenant between a husband and wife is out of order and perversion.

Perverted Leaders

A mentor of mine, John Maxwell says, "Everything hinges and falls on leadership." I could not agree more. We need great leaders to rise up and bring influence to nations and society at large. Quality leadership is needed in our churches and families as well. Unfortunately today leaders have lost credibility with those that follow them. Scandalous actions, control, manipulation and perversion has gripped many leaders into operating out of the wrong spirit.

Leadership starts with character not gifting. Many leaders are gifted and talented but they lack character. Character is critical, as it is the basis for standing strong in the mist of opposition, criticism and a culture than goes counter to the culture of the Kingdom of God. We need righteous leaders.

The bible says, *"when the godly are in authority, the people rejoice. But when the wicked are in power, they groan." (Proverbs 29:2 TLB)*

Because Jezebel hates authority, she will always target leaders. She will look to lure them into greed, control, power and position and get them to advance their man-made kingdoms rather than the Kingdom of God. Leaders are not to lord over people. They are not better than the people they are called to serve. They are simply gifts given whereby people can be guided and directed to live their lives pleasing to the Lord. Jesus said if you want to be a great leader, you must seek to serve.

Then they began to argue among themselves about who would be the greatest among them. Jesus told them, "In this world the kings and great men lord it over their people, yet they are called 'friends of the people.' But among you it will be different. Those who are the greatest among you should take the lowest rank, and the leader should be like a servant – Luke 22:24-25 (TLB)

A perverted leader is one that wants to be served by those that follow them.

We see this problem arising specifically in the spiritual fathering dimension of the church. Self-proclaimed spiritual fathers, using their sons and daughters as vehicles to advance their agenda by having gathered them up like livestock, goes against the original intention of the relationship. Genuine spiritual fathering is not about a son or daughter serving their father, but rather it's about the father serving them.

We need spiritual fathers in the church to raise up strong healthy disciples and sons and daughters. However the relationship must be based on biblical principles and not personal gain. Perversion arises when the son or daughter begins to idolize the leader and places more value on them than they do the truth of God's word. This has opened the door for perversion such as molestation, fornication, homosexuality, adultery and rape to gain a stronghold in our churches. Many organizations have become cesspools of perverted types and the righteous has become the minority.

Additionally, people in the most prominent places of leadership and influence are some of the most biblically illiterate people, and Jezebel utilizes their position of authority to deceive the people into thinking they should support and cover-up this behavior. These "religious players" have no real doctrinal foundation. Yet they utilize their charismatic charm and perversion into forming a soul tie with their followers. They excite crowds through playing on their emotions and demand allegiance by twisting and wrangling scripture. Many see what's happening, but out of fear of being ostracized by others they remain silent.

Other leaders know this is going on.

Many times perverted behaviors are looked over, swept under the rug and covered as not to "make the people stumble." They don't want to lose numbers and answer to the masses, so they keep secret counsel and call it restoration. The Jezebelic network is very strong in religious organizations and leaders are fearful that if they expose the sin that they will loose their ability to preach at another ministers' church or conference. Additionally, others wink at the perversion due the perverted leaders ability to generate large and handsome offerings

'Sexual' Perversions among Leaders

I personally have known of leaders that have engaged in perversion. Ranging from text messages to *"sisters"* that are nothing more than flirtatious sexual innuendos, to engaging in actual sexual intercourse with members of their flock. Many pay "hush money" as a means to cover for these perverted leaders girlfriends and boyfriends.

Another perversion is where these foul leaders guarantee promotion to aspiring ministers, psalmist, gospel artists and musicians by way of sexual (*heterosexual and homosexual*) favors. Many homosexuals meander around the church and are given titles and all access passes to the various functions of the church due to submission to the seductive Jezebel spirit operating in perverted leadership. Marketing executives' administrative assistants, adjutants, armor bearers, and sons are some of the cover names given by these wicked leaders for their boyfriends and mistresses. In some denominations and networks the

Jezebelic web is so tightly coiled that we now have secretaries to Pastors who don't mind "sharing" the Pastor with his wife and/or anyone else he may bring into his destructive web of perversion.

Incest and rape can also be found among perverted leaders. In one incident, a Pastor that was supposed to be helping a woman ended up raping her. This fragile woman was staying in a house the church owned. She had just gotten out of an abusive marriage; moved to another place with her three small children, simply to get a fresh start. This woman had a talent in the area of music, and the leader placed her into a position over the praise and worship in the local church. One night as she put her kids to bed and she herself looked to retire for the evening, stepped out of the shower and there he was. Obviously startled, she asked why he was there and how he got in. He held up his keys and told her nothing was free. He raped her! Unmoved by his cold, callous and perverted behavior, the leader demanded she continue to serve in her praise and worship responsibilities. The next day, while preaching, he kept calling her name out saying things like: "don't let the devil steal from you." Later he sent his cronies (deacons and elders i.e. thugs) to threaten and intimidate her, ultimately advising her that it was best that she be on her way and leave the city before "something happened" to her.

While these situations are not necessarily the "norm," they do happen. This is classic spiritual pride and perversion. Paul, the Apostle addressed this type of behavior in the 1st Century church at Corinth.

> "I also received a report of scandalous sex within your church family, a kind that wouldn't be tolerated even outside the church: One of your men is sleeping with his stepmother. And you're so above it all that it doesn't even faze you! Shouldn't this break your hearts? Shouldn't it bring you to your knees in tears? Shouldn't this person and his conduct be confronted and dealt with" – I Corinthians 5:1-2 (The Message Bible)

Sexual immorality is a growing trend in the church today. Not only in the pews but also in the pulpits. The spirit of Jezebel is behind this immoral movement, tapping into the lust of the flesh with its seductive agenda. It typically remains concealed by a tolerant spirit and goes unnoticed by delusional religious fanatics that fail to recognize the true Jezebel in operation because they have been seduced into the controlling web.

Unfortunately, there is a mindset in the religious culture that some subscribe to that has them continue to follow a leader that operates in perversion or error. Notice in the scripture below, that the blind leader doesn't fall by his self. Rather, both he and the blind that is following him fall into the pit together.

Let them alone: they be blind leaders of the blind. And if the blind lead the blind, both shall fall into the ditch –
Matthew 15:14

When speaking to the religious leaders of his day, Jesus advised the people to leave them alone and do not follow after them. Why do so many people follow leaders when they know of this perversion? It's incomprehensible.

Accountability needed

Clearly, we lack accountability in our churches. Leaders must be held accountable and responsible for their actions. The goal of addressing these perversions is not to slander or defame an individual, specifically a leader. Rather, we must expose the wickedness in anticipation of restoring the fallen leader and bringing an end to Jezebels controlling network. And what about the victim? People come to our churches to receive deliverance, healing and wholeness, not to be exploited and taken advantage of.

Paul goes on to tell us how to handle situations such as these:

"I'll tell you what I would do. Even though I'm not there in person, consider me right there with you, because I can fully see what's going on. I'm telling you that this is wrong. You must not simply look the other way and hope it goes away on its own. Bring it out in the open and deal with it in

the authority of Jesus our Master. Assemble the community—I'll be present in spirit with you and our Master Jesus will be present in power. Hold this man's conduct up to public scrutiny. Let him defend it if he can! But if he can't, then out with him! It will be totally devastating to him, of course, and embarrassing to you. But better devastation and embarrassment than damnation. You want him on his feet and forgiven before the Master on the Day of Judgment" – I Corinthians 5: 3-5 (The Message Bible)

God designed equipping centers as a place where spiritual leaders could watch out for the welfare of the saints. *(I Peter 5:1-4; Hebrews 13:17).* Leaders and believers who answer only to themselves can easily rationalize sinful attitudes or actions. Apostles, Prophets, Teachers, etc. are needed to perfect and equip the saints so they can do the work of serving others. Elders are needed to set things in order. When a believer is dis-engaged or disconnected they are dysfunctional, perverted in their thinking and will never excel. Accountability is critical to effectively measure success, provide gap analysis and to engage in process improvement techniques especially with young believers. Leaders need accountability to measure character and maintain credibility in the church.

We must maintain integrity and hold leaders to a higher standard. Exposure is not a bad thing – it's a biblical thing. Light must expose the dark workings of Jezebel's underworld. Her diabolical network of perversion must be destroyed. We can be silent on these issues no more. Paul said, *"deal with it."* Don't sweep it under the rug. Leaders, apostolic fathers and church overseers have a responsibility to guard the faith and contend with Jezebels perversions. No longer can we tolerate Jezebels perversion among our leaders.

Section Three
Jezebels Witchcrafts

Witchcraft and sorcery is forbidden in the scripture because of its association with demonic activities and the dark underworld. Sorcery is associated with practices of spiritualism *(2 Kings 23:24),* the spirit of harlotry *(Nahum. 3:4)* and idolatry *(Micah. 5:12).* During Jezebel's tenure as Queen over Israel, witchcraft was revived *(2 Kings 9:22)* and it has continued throughout history. Today we have much witchcraft in the church.

The Jezebel spirit is born out of witchcraft and rebellion. This ancient evil spirit is one of the most common spirits in operation today, both in the church and in the world, and it is a powerful enemy of the body of Christ. It operates in the minds of people everywhere and randomly navigates through churches and ministries by riding on the backs of sincere believers whose hearts are for God.

Witchcraft is a spirit that attacks nations, families, cities and ministries alike. It is an ancient evil outlaw that has been already been judged, yet continues to operate covertly. Yes, witchcraft dwells among us. It has bombarded and invaded churches everywhere. At its core is the spirit of religion. It is the founding spirit behind the 30,000 denominations in Christianity alone. It has used gospel music as a platform to mesmerize spiritual groupies and release sexual perversion within its culture. Witchcraft employs Christians throughout the world as its mouthpiece.

As breakthrough believers and apostolic governing ministries we are called to challenge with the evil forces of witchcraft that provide support to the ancient witch – Jezebel. Jezebel has perpetrated and penetrated our churches. She is a spirit that disguises herself as a spiritual progressive that knows how to flow and move by the spirit. Her highly camouflaged operation is blind to most people. Many of God's people are not aware of the flood of witchcraft upon our nation, families and people groups.

The spirit of witchcraft dominates and uses numerous distribution channels. Hollywood, Music, Arts and Entertainment, Education, Government, Business and Religion are just some to mention. It has created a naked, open and liberal society. It has moved an entire generation away from the commandments of God, so that it can participate in the works of darkness.

When there is sexual promiscuity (fornication, homosexuality, molestation, rape, abortion,, fantasy lust (rejection) and pornography) in society there is witchcraft in operation. Today we not only are witnessing sexual perversion increasing, but there is also an increase in the worship of idols and pagan gods. There is a strong connection between idolatry and sexual perversions. This is all birthed out of witchcraft.

Witchcraft can be released through many activities such as spells, charms, chants, the occult, drugs, potions, amulets and prophetic fortune telling. However, there is no greater way to release witchcraft then through one's tongue. Witchcraft is a deadly poison that isolates, and inebriates its victim.

> *But the tongue can no man tame; it is an unruly evil, full of deadly poison – James 3:8*

Witchcraft discriminates against no one. It attacks churches, families, marriages and friendships. It operates in white people, black people and any other race you can think of. It is a spirit that works through male and female genders. It works through the saints, the sinner, the laity and clergy. Witchcraft is a very common spirit in operation today. When thinking about witchcraft, do not be tricked into the Hollywood mindset of an ugly woman, riding on a broom while dressed in black clothing. No, witchcraft operates much more subtle than this.

Witchcraft is the work (craft) of a witch being carried out. It is a spiritual force behind the witch. Witchcraft is also a work of the flesh that attacks your mind. The primary target of witchcraft is – the Mind. When the flesh has not been crucified (*daily*) then it has a greater susceptibility to fall prey to witchcrafts diabolical escapades.

> *O You poor and silly and thoughtless and unreflecting and senseless Galatians! Who has fascinated <u>or bewitched or cast a spell over</u> you, unto whom—right before your very eyes—Jesus Christ (the Messiah) was openly and graphically set forth and portrayed as crucified? Let me ask you this one question: Did you receive the [Holy] Spirit as the result of obeying the Law and doing its works, or was it by hearing [the message of the Gospel] and believing [it]? [Was it from observing a law of rituals or from a message of faith? Are you so foolish and so senseless and so silly? Having begun [your new life spiritually] with the [Holy] Spirit, are you now reaching perfection [by dependence] on <u>the flesh</u> – Galatians 3:1-3 Amplified Version*

As you can see from the above scripture, Paul the Apostle ties the flesh to witchcraft. In the same letter in the 5th division, Paul goes on to tell the Galatians ….

> *Now the works of the flesh are manifest, which are these; Adultery, fornication, uncleanness, lasciviousness, Idolatry, **witchcraft,** hatred, variance, emulations, wrath, strife, seditions, heresies, Envyings, murders, drunkenness, revellings, and such like: of the which I tell you before, as I have also told you in time past, that they which do such things shall not inherit the kingdom of God – Galatians 5:19-21*

The evil of witchcraft is revealed in the dependence on the flesh and profound disobedience to the will of God. Where you find witchcraft you'll find the flesh and vice-a-versa. Witchcraft works among those that do not walk according to the Spirit. To walk in the Spirit is to live a life of obedience to the word of God, You cannot walk in the Spirit and obey your flesh.

The flesh is diametrically opposed to the Kingdom of Heaven. The Kingdom is the rule, reign, authority and dominion of God. Therefore, the flesh resists the Kingdom and is rebellious to King Jesus Himself. The flesh and Spirit cannot mix. It is impossible to walk in the flesh and Spirit simultaneously. When you walk in the flesh you subsequently open the door to witchcraft attacks. Walking in the flesh is a decision you make and when you do, the Spirit man, the New Man in you, is effectively shut down and not able to do the things that you would.

For the flesh lusteth against the Spirit, and the Spirit against the flesh: and these are contrary the one to the other: so that ye cannot do the things that ye would –
Galatians 5:17

When a believer is walking in the flesh they are operating in witchcraft. Witchcraft is Rebellion (ref: *I Samuel 15:23*).

Rebellious people are susceptible to hosting the sprit of

Jezebel. Rebellion is witchcraft and Jezebel was birthed out of witchcraft. Rebellion creates the perfect environment for Jezebel to release her witchcrafts.

And it came to pass, when Joram saw Jehu, that he said, Is it peace, Jehu? And he answered, What peace, so long as the whoredoms of thy mother Jezebel and her witchcrafts are so many – II Kings 9:22

What is the Flesh?

The flesh is the carnal mindset. It is the old nature based on a mindset that is in opposition to the things of God. The flesh is not of God but rather of Satan.

But when Jesus turned and looked at his disciples, he rebuked Peter. "Get behind me, Satan!" he said. "You do not have in mind the concerns of God, but merely human concerns – Mark 8:33 (NIV)

When you are not mindful of the things of God, when your priority is not the Kingdom (the rule and government) of God, then you are walking in the flesh. Today many Christians are born again and citizens of the Kingdom of God. By the mere fact that they have confessed with their mouth and believe in their heart, (*Romans 10:9-10*) their names are written in the Lambs book of Life. However, just because one is born-again, doesn't necessarily mean that they're "walking in the Spirit."

Additionally, some think that they can live in the Spirit without complete and non-negotiable obedience to the Word of God. This is delusion and concrete evidence that supports the fact that they walk in the flesh. Obedience to God's word through the renewing of the mind is vital in maintaining deliverance of one's soul (mind, will and emotions.)

Believers that do not renew their minds with the Word of God and are constantly satisfying the cravings of the flesh are prime targets and suspects when it comes to harboring Jezebel. Believers that are double-minded and do not seek the Kingdom of God are unstable souls. Walking in and out of flesh (or spirit) is spiritual schizophrenia. You cannot serve the carnal mind and the mind of the spirit. That which is Spirit is Spirit and that which is Flesh is Flesh.

For they that are after the flesh do mind the things of the flesh; but they that are after the Spirit the things of the Spirit. For to be carnally minded is death; but to be spiritually minded is life and peace. Because the carnal mind is enmity against God: for it is not subject to the law of God, neither indeed can be. So then they that are in the flesh cannot please God – Romans 8:5-8

Jezebel attacks and uses unstable souls.

Having eyes full of adultery, and that cannot cease from sin; beguiling unstable souls .... – 2 Peter 2:14

When the mind is not renewed it becomes and open door for the lies and deceptions of Jezebel. When emotions are uncontrolled or remain in an undelivered state, Jezebel will seduce her prey into her bed of perversion. When the will does not desire the righteousness of God, Jezebel will commit fornication with God's servants.

The instability of one's soul (mind, will and emotions) provides a safe haven for Jezebel. Make no mistake about it, Jezebel will release her spells against you if you are unstable in your walk with God or ignorant of whom you are in Christ.

.... my people are destroyed from lack of knowledge. – Hosea 4:6 (NIV)

Therefore if any man be in Christ, he is a new creature: old things are passed away; behold, all things are become new. – 2 Corinthians 5:17

Believer's that struggle with an identity crisis due to an un-renewed mind are prime targets for Jezebel's witchcrafts to gain a stronghold in their lives.

The topic of witchcraft is so vast and complex that we simply do not have enough space in this Book to talk about it in detail. However it is my (the author) desire to elaborate on the more subtle and modern revision of how witchcraft works in the 21st-century. Specifically in our churches and families.

Witchcraft in the 21st Century

Witchcraft released in the 21st century is typically done by way of spoken "evil" words against others. These are commonly referred to as word curses. The power of one's words is remarkable. The word of God tells us that; *Death and life are in the power of the tongue (Proverbs 18:21).* Many Christians today engage in the craft of witches unknowingly by speaking negativity, gossip, slander, controlling prayers and prophetic words of manipulation.

Toxic words of witchcraft spoken against you can release demonic assignments against your life. These assignments become fortified when spells and hexes are received through the feeble and weak-minded. Words can be used to bless or curse. As believers, we are instructed to bless, and curse not *(ref Romans 12:24).* Unfortunately after 1700 years of the religious spirit controlling the direction of the church, a demonic system has been created whereby carnally minded believers feel justified in releasing words a of witchcraft against their brother or sister.

The importance of the words used (in witchcraft) when casting a spell cannot be underestimated or overemphasized. Words are critical to the effectiveness of witchcraft. When toxic words are spoken it's important to remember that the words must conjure up an emotional response. Witchcraft released against you binds you and generates its greatest results when the emotions are compromised. To accomplish this, the focus of the Jezebelic host is not necessarily the literal words spoken, but rather the way that the words are spoken. The reason for this is to create an emotional attachment where a spiritual soul tie can be formed.

Jezebel is attracted to those who have unstable minds that developed through prior attacks of witchcraft against them. These prior attacks, over a period of time, successfully created a stronghold in their soul, specifically the emotional arena. A stronghold is a fortified place. It is a dwelling place for demons. Demons refer to this stronghold as *"their house."* *(ref Lk 11:24)* Demonic strongholds can remain in a state of hibernation. Over time, and when a word is <u>released</u>, the witchcraft in a person will "trigger" and activate. The interesting thing about this is that the word <u>released</u> isn't necessarily an evil word. Again, it's not what was said but rather how it was received. If you've ever experienced a time where you had a discussion with someone, or perhaps you were preaching a group of people, and although you had the best intention, someone took what you said the wrong way? The next thing you know they're manifesting accusation against you by saying things such as, *'you offended them.'* This is due to Jezebelic witchcraft's ability to distort and confuse the minds of believers. Once the target takes an offense, witchcraft binds the mind, and the stronghold quickly moves from a relapsed condition to a progressive condition.

So, the point is, witchcraft is both released against the saints, and carried by them as hosts. At times, we see this in the arena of prayer, intercession and prophetic utterances. I have personally witnessed multiple accounts of witchcraft in operation during these times. The line is thin, but with proper training and spiritual discernment, you can learn how to identify witchcraft.

Let me first give you an example of a normal (good) prayer:

"Father, I pray for my husband and that your love touches his heart and is manifested throughout his life."

Now, in contrast, here is a prayer of witchcraft:

"Lord, please make my husband start treating me right and show him just how bad he treats me"

Prayers like this are commonly referred to as witchcraft prayers because it's like you're trying to speak incantations over a person to conjure up the result you want. Many times these witchcraft prayers are nothing more than retaliatory responses to compensate for the abuse and pain experienced in one's life. Witchcraft prayers are words prayed out of a desire to manipulate the will of another person. Christian witchcraft is when one uses a decree and their spiritual authority to override another person's will. Witchcraft is the control of others and imposing one's will upon others, usually with the goal of achieving a negative result. Witchcraft places its victim in significant bondage.

Witchcraft looks to **dominate** and **control** you so that you will not think for yourself. It will use criticism and accusation as primary weapons to beat you into submission. Individuals who inappropriately complain about church leaders, the actions of the church, and pressure others within the church to conform to their desires are operating out of witchcraft. Watch for those who conjure up strife and discord among the church body as they stealthily tiptoe around. They will always look for you to be a 'soundboard' for their complaints. Never listen to them and quickly terminate the conversation. The spirit of Jezebel working in them is luring you into a trap in an attempt to get you in agreement with them.

Witchcraft will utilize **intimidation** as a demonic tactic. Have you ever been around a person that made you feel small, insignificant or irrelevant? That's witchcraft. Intimidating witchcraft often comes from someone that is in a position of authority. It is the handling of that authority in a perverted manner that makes it witchcraft. One should never use their position of authority to intimidate others into accepting or rejecting what is said or done. Additionally, some can become so intimidated by others that they never make a decision without the person who is operating in witchcrafts approval. Anytime you feel that your will and decision-making faculties have been compromised, it's most likely witchcraft.

The use of position or power to direct the outcome of something that is in line with fleshly desires rather than Kingdom mandates and the leading of the Holy Spirit is manipulation. **Manipulation** is a form of witchcraft and is designed to control the outcome of people and things. Witchcraft works very strongly through manipulative controllers that are usually very close to you. The more one who operates in witchcraft gets to knows you, the easier it will be for them to control you. This includes parents, children, siblings, bosses, church leaders and best friends.

Demonic controllers are on assignment to waste an excessive amount of your time. They will steal all of your discretionary time, and look to invade in restrictive areas also. Witchcraft will keep you busy in activities yet never accomplish anything in your life. Witchcraft and religion go hand-in-hand. This is why we see in the religious churches a lot of activities going on, yet no one ever achieves any measurable and impactful results. It's the classic gerbil on the treadmill. A lot of energy is expended, yet he never gets anywhere. When you're busy doing a lot of activities and tasks, yet feel is though you've never moved out of the current situation or condition you're in, that is most likely a spirit of witchcraft that has been released against your mind.

Witchcraft will go out of the way to control and waste your time. Witchcraft controllers spend abnormal amounts of time with their victims. Be careful of people who connect to you and consumed vast amounts of your time. This can be either in person, on the telephone or through social media. It's commonly done through dramatic events that are manufactured to create a tether with your emotions, leaving with a sense that you need to fix other people's problems. Leaders must be especially careful not to engage in meetings where people want to come in and make them nothing more than a demonic sounding board.

If you've ever been around a person that has had a discussion with you for any length of time and when you've concluded the conversation you've walked away exhausted, depleted, lacking energy and at times a throbbing headache, it is most likely the direct result of witchcraft being released in your life.

Common symptoms when under the spell of witchcraft

Are you under the spell of witchcraft? Have you been targeted by Christian word curses? Some of the symptoms of witchcraft attacking your life manifest in numerous ways. A few of those are:

- Confusion
- Loss of memory
- Depression
- Fatigue
- Feeling drained
- Lack of motivation
- Procrastination
- A desire to quit
- Suicidal thoughts
- Drifting
- Headaches/Migraines
- Extreme pain in the eyes, neck and temple areas
- Nervousness
- Numerous miscarriages
- Inordinate sexual relationships
- Questioning your purpose

Some other feelings you may experience when a spirit of witchcraft has been release against you are:

- The need to be unattached, distanced and isolated from:

    - The Body of Christ
    - Friends

- Family
- Leaders / those in authority
- Those that speak truth to you

- Fear [that others are talking about you]
- Insecurity
- Inferiority
- Rejection
- Bitterness
- Loss of Joy
- Slothful & Lazy
- Anger
- Frustrated
- Intolerant of others
- Irritable
- Anxiety
- Worry
- Trouble sleeping
- Loss of Libido

When witchcraft is present and prevalent, people will do things and gravitate to things without even understanding why they do it. The effects of witchcraft are very similar to that of being stuck in a matrix. You're in it and working, yet you really have no focus. Witchcraft is a spirit that will cause a person to be unfocused. Have you ever been in a situation where you responded to things or acted out things, yet, you really didn't understand precisely why you did what you did? This could be due to witchcraft that has been released against you. In my many years of deliverance ministry, I have counseled numerous people that have engaged in perverted activities, ranging from lying to sexual promiscuity. When asking these people, why they did it, many simply said they felt there was some type of force against them that demanded they do it. This is classic witchcraft and the spirit of Jezebel in operation.

Witchcraft is a spirit that keeps people blind to the simplest tasks and functions in life. Those affected by witchcraft often struggle with their memory. Forgetfulness of the simplest things such as names, lock combinations, birthdays and what they ate for lunch are very common. When witchcraft is released against people they have a hard time concentrating. They also drift. They're often in a hypnotic state whereby they are unable to make any significant contribution to life.

Witchcraft sucks the life out of you

One of the leading indicators of being attacked by a spirit of witchcraft is fatigue. Many who are under the spell of a witch through negative and evil words released against them will find that their energy and strength has been depleted. They typically feel tired, exhausted, depressed and may experience heaviness in their chest or rapid breathing.

When one is targeted by witchcraft, they can feel emotionally drained or debilitated and often physically sick. When witchcraft is released against you it doesn't matter how much exercise you get, the shots of espresso you consume, the number of vitamins you take, or the healthy-balanced diet you have. It will not help. If you feel tired all the time, beware; witchcraft is most likely in operation. I know of people that have experienced this to the utmost. They have gone to the doctor only to be told that they have no idea what's wrong with them. They've consumed enormous amounts of energy drinks yet continue to be exhausted. Many find that sleeping 10 and 12 hours makes no dent in this exhaustion. They even wake up tired. This is classic Jezebel and clearly a spirit of witchcraft in operation.

Witchcraft causes depression

One of the other signs of witchcraft that one must be on guard for is depression. When one is exhausted and fatigue, depression can easily set in. Witchcraft plays on your mind and will begin to speak to you. A person who is victimized by fatigue and exhaustion make come to a place where they become depressed due to their lack of achievements in life. Jezebelic witches, through the release of word curses, launch cannon balls of stress and anxiety towards their targets. Many, when visiting their family physician, are prescribed anti-depressant drugs. While taking certain medications are understandable and have there place in the recovery process of various sicknesses, ailments and injuries, one must be extremely careful that they do not fall into an addictive state, whereby witchcraft can further gain a stronghold. Breakthrough believers must be on guard and have their minds renewed so they do not accept this spirit.

Addictions

Another sign of witchcraft in operation is to participate in various addictions. Prescription and OTC drugs, illegal drugs, alcohol, tobacco (*smoking and chewing*) is some of the addictions that may exist when one is under the influence of witchcraft.

Witchcraft is the Greek word: *"pharmakeia."* It is where we get the word "pharmaceuticals." It speaks of medication, and (by extension) magic, sorcery and witchcraft. Witchcraft may be involved in the use or the administering of drugs. Pharmakeia (drugs) is one of the many strategies of Jezebel. When addicted to drugs, alcohol, tobacco and weed, Jezebel (Satan) has the advantage over us! Addictions provide the perfect cover for all Jezebels dark strategies to destroy lives, nations and races.

Sexual addictions and perversion such as pornography, promiscuity, multiple partners, sexting, homosexuality, lesbianism, and chronic masturbation are other indicators of a witchcraft spell being release against you.

Isolation

Witchcraft is an isolating spirit that lures people away from those who can truly speak into their lives. Jezebel tag teams with witchcraft and the power of isolation to separate her victims from positive relationships, genuine apostolic fathers and anointed churches. Witchcraft needs to separate and isolate its victim from the influence of church leaders, family and loved ones in order to be most effective.

Witchcraft isolates it's prey and keeps them away from those who are bold and Kingdom-minded. It also isolates you from those who genuinely love you. If you find yourself connected to a person that is unwilling to share you with anyone, specifically with anointed leaders, this could be a sign of witchcraft brewing against you.

Witchcraft will do whatever it takes to control the environment around it. Those who operate in witchcraft use their powers to isolate their victims and turn you into a loner. People that do not associate with others and tend to ostracize themselves from society may be under the curse of witchcraft. Those that live in a world where they're typically alone could be under the power of witchcraft. Those who are fearful of socializing with others, or are afraid of crowds, could be under the spell of a witch. Finally, those who are found hibernating and being alone may have succumbed to the power of witchcraft.

False Holy Spirit

Another sign of witchcraft in the church is a false holy spirit. A false Holy Spirit is a move that some have embraced out of their need to appease the flesh. It is a demonic spirit that excites us, but does not transform us. It is incapable of helping one to overcome anything, and does not draw you closer to God, but makes you feel you are.

A false holy spirit takes your peace and joy, replacing it with an energy that promotes anxiety and busyness. It takes away your interest in the Word of God and moves you towards social activity, sensationalism and excitableness. It is powerless of producing holy behavior, and genuine and heavenly worship. It has no authority to overcome evil or bring one into the presence of God. A false holy spirit perpetuates the churches lukewarmness by destroying the hunger for truth and righteousness. It recruits its followers through spooky, weird, bizarre manifestations, all done in the name of the Lord. Its wonders are false, and its oil is clouded with perversion.

Many will say to Me on that day, Lord, Lord, have we not prophesied in Your name and driven out demons in Your name and done many mighty works in Your name? And then I will say to them openly (publicly), I never knew you; depart from Me, you who act wickedly [disregarding My commands]. – Matthew 7:21-22 (Amplified Version)

False Tongues

A false tongue is birth out of a counterfeit holy spirit. There is a real Holy Spirit that releases the weight of God's glory and presence of the Lord. Yet the counterfeit is one that is focused on pleasing the flesh. It is an entertainment spirit that draws attention to self. This is something that believers must guard for, as it has invaded our churches and has largely gone undetected.

False tongues is a trick of Satan to entertain our attention away from the true work of the Holy Spirit, which is the magnification and exaltation of Jesus Christ, and get people side tracked by focusing on the gifts. When people become so engrossed with the gifts that they forget the gift-giver and prime priority, (the Kingdom) it will also open the door to witchcraft and perversion.

When discerning false tongues there are some things to watch out for. Clearly, just because a person has one or more indicators does not guarantee that they are operating in witchcraft. The main question is, "what spirit are they operating out of?" To properly ascertain that requires discernment and proper exegesis of scripture. However here are some things to beware of:

Strange and Weird behavior when speaking in tongues.

An example would be body contortions, uncontrollable twerking, shaking and yelling when speaking in tongues.

Speaking in tongues when a person in having demons cast out of them.

Demons do not have the ability to interpret "other tongues." Additionally, when tongues are released publicly, the word of God instructs us that there must be an interpreter. Without an interpreter, the door to confusion is open. Witchcraft and confusion always work together. I see this a lot with people conducting deliverance ministry with people. They yell at the deliverance candidate in tongues. This practice is not necessary when liberating people through deliverance ministry.

Demonically possessed people speaking in tongues and laughing

When engaged in deliverance ministry you must be careful when demonically bound host begins to speak in tongues. Tongues are a "gift" of the Holy Spirit and operate as He wills. There is no purpose in a demonically bound person who is being ministered to by a deliverance minister to speak in tongues during the "ejecting" process. This behavior is self-seeking, brings confusion and contention.

> *But if you have bitter jealousy (envy) and contention (rivalry, selfish ambition) in your hearts, do not pride yourselves on it and thus be in defiance of and false to the Truth.*
>
> *This [superficial] wisdom is not such as comes down from above, but is earthly, unspiritual (animal), even devilish (demoniacal) – James 3:14-15 (Amplified Version)*

There have been times where I've had others who were severely bound laugh hysterically during the deliverance process. It's as if they were intoxicated and unable to focus. While some charismatic believers may look at his as a sign of deliverance or breakthrough, I have called out many "mocking demons" in operation sent to discredit and lessen the positive effects of deliverance ministry. Remember, deliverance ministry is not flaky, spooky, weird or some out of control activity.

Manifestations, sensations and demonstrations of a False Holy Spirit (witchcraft)

- Uncontrollable laughing
- Spontaneous vocalization of animal sounds
- Jerking, shaking, rolling and slithering on the floor
- Itching, vibrating, prickling, tingling, stinging or crawling sensations
- Intense sensation of heat or cold
- Muscle twitches, spasms, cramps and convulsions
- Energy rushes, electricity circulating in the body
- Arousal and orgasms during worship

- Postures or moving one's body in unusual ways
- Mental confusion, difficulty concentrating and altered states of consciousness
- Psychic and extrasensory perception.
- Mass "slayings" of people in the "spirit"
- Direct awareness and guidance inner voices

Witchcraft in our churches fly's under the radar mostly because it appears to be spiritual. Many that operate in witchcraft look mystical, sound spiritual, sensationalize everything and have a form of godliness.

Having a form of godliness, but denying the power thereof: from such turn away – 2 Timothy 3:5

The shenanigans of witchcraft, which many people considered to be "super spiritual" are designed to manipulate you. Have you ever had a conversation with someone that acted in a manner that some may consider "ultra-spiritual?" I mean where you can't even have a normal conversation with the person without them moving in and out of *"spiritual wonderland."* As you're talking to them they appear to be in some deep thought, yet their attention is not towards you. When they begin to converse with you, they may go from English to speaking in an unknown tongue. Or perhaps they spiritualize the smallest fact. I have had times where talking to someone has become an event rather than a discussion. Their body has jerk back-and-forth as they spoke on the smallest of things. Or, their statement that could have been a few syllables ended up being a 20-minute conversation that went one way– their way.

When witchcraft is an operation this is a tactic that's designed to manipulate and intimidate you. It's as if the person wants to get the upper hand on you spiritually. Ultimately this is designed to control you in limit your identity of who you are. Witchcraft will make you feel that without the person operating in this demonic spirit you have no personal identity of your own.

People releasing witchcraft will often get spiritual with you by finishing their conversation speaking in tongues or some super spiritual cliché. People who walk in witchcraft have an air of spiritual superiority about them.

Witchcraft gravitates to apostolic-prophetic churches

Because of the liberty that exists in apostolic-prophetic churches, witchcraft and Jezebel in particular, love to hangout in these gatherings. Jezebel hungers for the microphone and releases word curses camouflaged under the prophetic anointing. Remember, Jezebel calls herself a prophetess. I have seen many times where prophetic witchcraft is release by Jezebel or one of her prophets. Yes, Jezebel has her own prophets:

Now therefore send, and gather to me all Israel unto

mount Carmel, and the prophets of Baal four hundred and fifty, and the prophets of the groves four hundred, which eat at Jezebel's table – I Kings 18:19

Those that eat at Jezebel's table are the prophets of witchcraft. Baal is the god of prophetic divination. This spirit ushers people into idolatry under the disguise of religion.

Jezebel targets people that flow in the prophetic.

Jezebel loves personal prophecy and will use it as a vehicle to release her witchcraft and sorcery. Believers that do not submit to apostolic governmental authority and proper New Testament prophetic operations are high on the list of being used by witchcraft. Proper training in the prophetic and discernment is paramount in identifying potential Jezebel networks from being formed.

Jezebel will prophesy manipulative words over a person's life and combine it with utterances in false tongues. Jezebel has the ability to sound ultra-spiritual and commonly uses a mystical approach when engaged in her witchcrafts. Jezebel hates genuine and pure prophetic ministry because she detests the voice of God. She will pull out every trick available to block the prophetic dimension from functioning effectively.

Jezebel will look to kill genuine prophetic ministry and raise up prophetic sects through deception. Once deceived through Jezebel's trickeries, the host will commence to release witchcraft through controlling prayers and false prophetic unction's and spells. Jezebel is a thief and a robber that steals from people through religious manipulation and prophetic witchcraft.

Witchcraft is primarily released through words and Jezebel loves to talk. She will sound ultra-spiritual in her prophetic sorcery. The Jezebel spirit will play with the name of God and use it as a novelty by excessively using terms such as, *"God told me,"* or *"I saw this"* and *"I heard the spirit say."* Remember, just because someone says its God, doesn't mean it is God.

Jezebel and her witchcrafts are attracted to prophetic personalities and Pentecostal and Charismatic churches. I'm hearing of converted divinators testifying of practicing witches being implanted and infiltrating local church bodies, especially the charismatic-prophetic churches. Many of them are motivated by the kingdom of darkness to turn people away from the truth of God's word. This is why we have people popping up all over the place claiming to be a prophet, sent by God.

And when they had gone through the isle unto Paphos, they found a certain sorcerer, a false prophet, a Jew, whose name was Barjesus .... But Elymas the sorcerer (for so is *his name by interpretation) withstood them, **seeking to turn away** the deputy from the faith – Acts 13:6,8 (emphasis the author)*

Some Prophetic churches have become sorcerer boot camps where Jezebel sends her prophets to train and pervert the genuine prophetic gift. These prophetic sorcerers' affectionately release accusations, judgments and false words to the body. They have a strong desire to embed themselves into a leadership capacity and get particularly close to the set-leader. The reason for this is to control the flow of spiritual activities and create a dependency on the perceived "prophet."

Witchcraft embedded in the Prophetic, looks for opportunities to usurp authority and carry out its rebellious agenda. Watch for prophets, prophetic companies and prophetic intercessors that have self-promoting agendas. These agendas are rooted in the body of Christ and our local church bodies to bring confusion, chaos and division.

I personally recall a time where a group of witches camouflaging as "prophetic intercessors, strategically positioned themselves as spiritual watchmen called to protect the Apostles from the diabolical works of the enemy. Apparently, they felt that is was necessary for them to attend the conference so they could block the enemy from attacking the meeting. This "team," pranced around the conference giving random prophecies, telling outrageous and mysterious stories and hanging around key leaders looking for their "gifting" and "name" to be recognized and affirmed. Their prayers of witchcraft left many with extreme headaches, nausea and confusion. Many of them looked lost, dark and feeble. Their spooky costumes and religious paraphernalia only overshadowed their sunken eye sockets and frail appearance. Their hidden agenda was to be seen with VIP's and capture as many photo opportunities as possible.

Several months after the event I had a Sr. Pastor at a respectable church call me. After introducing himself, be began to tell me of a group of "female intercessors" that were from his ministry that attended our apostolic conference. As our discussion progressed, I discerned that this Pastor was emotionally shaken and distraught. He went on to tell me that when these band of prophetic intercessors returned to their home church, they quickly moved among the congregation telling the gullible that they had received a "special" impartation and that "God" was calling them to be Apostles. They successfully were able to hoodwink half of the congregation to leave this Pastors ministry and follow them. This is classic witchcraft birthed out of rebellion and inspired by a controlling Jezebel spirit.

Since this time, we continue to "mark them" as a gang of witches and warn others. Yet many will not heed to the warnings as people are drawn to the circus-like spiritual antics and mystical prophetic performances. Unfortunately the weary Pastor went into deep depression and has never truly recovered.

Much of this gains a foothold in apostolic-prophetic communities due to the carefree attitude in the church. The bottom line is, we have a culture in our churches where anything and everything goes. Additionally, we are critically lacking in the amount of Prophetic training in existence today. Much of what is considered quality equipping in this dimension is taught from an Old Testament view. This creates a fundamental gap in properly comprehending the office of a Prophet as well as the administration and operation of the prophetic gift, vis-à-vis the Holy Spirit.

Apostles and apostolic personnel that understand the Kingdom of God must govern prophetic churches and networks. Religious personnel are useless and defenseless against the craft of the witch.

Witchcraft partners with religious churches

Witchcraft is attracted to religious entertainment centers. The more religious a church is; the more witchcraft will prevail within it. Religious bishops, pastors and other leaders partner with Jezebel and protect her witchcraft from being exposed by releasing a spirit of fear among the flock. Watch for leaders and churches that impose heavy religious yokes on the people, specifically in the area of giving. A remark from the pulpit such as: "if you do not tithe, then you are cursed," is and example of religious control through fear.

Witchcraft is more common in churches than the average leader understands. It is primarily released through words, and Jezebel is slaughtering ministries by releasing word curses and casting spells on them. As Jezebel wiggles herself into positions of the leadership team, she will initiate a campaign of accusations against others on the team. Accusation is a fundamental weapon of Jezebel that gets its momentum from religion. The religious Pharisees of the 1st century were constantly looking to accuse Jesus and His followers. In like manner, the religious spirit deployed by Jezebel will look to assassinate genuine apostolic and prophetic leaders and ministry.

Jezebel will have religious people look more at outward appearance. As such, they have a propensity to exalt the flesh and suppress the spirit. This is why it's so important to get out of religious indoctrination centers.

Get free from the affect of Witchcraft

The fight against witchcraft and sorcery is a spiritual one, and those who hope to win must arm themselves with the sword of the spirit as Paul instructs believers in Ephesians:

And take the helmet of salvation, and the sword of the Spirit, which is the word of God – Ephesians 6:17

Today, more than ever, we must take the position of the mighty Jehu.

And it came to pass, when Joram saw Jehu, that he said, Is it peace, Jehu? And he answered, What peace, so long as the whoredoms of thy mother Jezebel and her <u>witchcrafts</u> are so many – 2 Kings 9:22

Jezebel and her witchcrafts were ultimately dismantled by several of her eunuchs at the order of Jehu. It is time for the prophets and citizens of the Kingdom of God to unite against this evil spirit masquerading in our churches. Under the anointing of the Holy Spirit, let us arise in the indignation of Jehu, and cast Jezebel and witchcraft down!

Other Books by Apostle Robert Summers

Deliverance Training Manual ©

It's about Time

Genuine Fathers – Willing Sons ©

Kingdom Principles of Success, Wealth & Prosperity ©

Harboring the Spirit of Jezebel ©

Gossip – The Weapon of Mass Destruction ©

Throw Jezebel Down ©

For a complete listing of resources please visit www.summersministries.com

Made in the USA
Middletown, DE
20 September 2018